We are rapidly reaching the limits of what our planet and its ecosystems can tolerate. To safeguard our natural ecosystems and enhance the resilience of our economies and societies, we need impact entrepreneurship that goes beyond merely maximizing shareholder returns at any cost by also seeking to generate benefits for people and the planet. But how can entrepreneurs build sustainability and profit missions into their business models without sacrificing profits? This book provides an excellent set of cases to illustrate how entrepreneurial businesses can combine their sustainability and resilience missions with their profit mission, thereby converting those missions from profit drags into profit drivers.

Erkko Autio, FBA

Professor of Technology Venturing and Entrepreneurship

Imperial College Business School, UK

One of the biggest challenges entrepreneurs often face is going from an innovative idea to finding how the innovation can be applied to benefit potential markets. Part of this challenge includes developing a business model that helps identify those potential markets, assess the potential demand in those markets, and ultimately assess the ability to sustain any business derived from the application of the innovation. In this well-written book, the authors have provided several interesting stories of innovations, the challenges faced and addressed by the innovators, and the business models that helped to make the innovations a success. In addition, the authors provide their own insights gained with each innovation story, which helps to provide valuable context for the reader/entrepreneur. In all innovations, "reinventing the wheel" can be costly and time consuming, and this book offers several real-world experiences that are sure to help any entrepreneur in their quest to make their great ideas more than just ideas. I highly recommend spending some time with this book!

Brian Janz, Ph.D.
Professor of Management Information Systems
and Past Innovator-in-Residence
The University of Memphis, USA

PIONEERING
A SMART,
SUSTAINABLE,
AND
RESILIENT
FUTURE

**Founder Stories
and Business Models**

PIONEERING
A SMART,
SUSTAINABLE,
AND
RESILIENT
FUTURE

Founder Stories
and Business Models

Chiraphol N Chiyachantana
Tamas Makany
David K Ding

Singapore Management University, Singapore

World Scientific

NEW JERSEY · LONDON · SINGAPORE · BEIJING · SHANGHAI · HONG KONG · TAIPEI · CHENNAI · TOKYO

Published by

World Scientific Publishing Co. Pte. Ltd.

5 Toh Tuck Link, Singapore 596224

USA office: 27 Warren Street, Suite 401-402, Hackensack, NJ 07601

UK office: 57 Shelton Street, Covent Garden, London WC2H 9HE

Library of Congress Cataloging-in-Publication Data
Names: Chiyachantana, Chiraphol N., author. | Makany, Tamas, author. |
  Ding, David K., 1959- author.
Title: Pioneering a smart, sustainable, and resilient future : founder stories and business models /
  Chiraphol N Chiyachantana, Singapore Management University, Singapore,
  Tamas Makany, Singapore Management University, Singapore, and
  David K Ding, Singapore Management University, Singapore.
Description: New Jersey : World Scientific, [2024] | Includes bibliographical references.
Identifiers: LCCN 2023020422 | ISBN 9789811267901 (hardcover) |
  ISBN 9789811267918 (ebook for institutions) | ISBN 9789811267925 (ebook for individuals)
Subjects: LCSH: Entrepreneurship. | Business planning. | Sustainable development.
Classification: LCC HB615 .C6273 2024 | DDC 658.4/21--dc23/eng/20230616
LC record available at https://lccn.loc.gov/2023020422

British Library Cataloguing-in-Publication Data
A catalogue record for this book is available from the British Library.

For any available supplementary material, please visit
https://www.worldscientific.com/worldscibooks/10.1142/13187#t=suppl

Desk Editors: Nimal Koliyat/Thaheera Althaf/Kura Sunaina

Typeset by Stallion Press
Email: enquiries@stallionpress.com

Foreword

As a city-state with no natural resources, Singapore has relied on the resourcefulness and resilience of Singaporeans to seize, create, and grow opportunities out of our constraints and challenges. The Singapore story is one of innovation and entrepreneurship exercised at every level — government, businesses, and individuals.

Innovation and entrepreneurship are more relevant than ever today, in Singapore and around the world, as challenges become more diverse and complex. Fostering innovation must first begin with nurturing an entrepreneurial spirit in our people, especially among the young, to find opportunities in challenges, and to have the gumption to pioneer fresh solutions for the world.

Over successive editions, the Lee Kuan Yew Global Business Plan Competition (LKYGBPC) has given students and youth in Singapore and around the world the opportunity to pitch their start-ups to business leaders, venture capitalists, and companies. In turn, these investors and companies get to work with the brightest young talents and their innovations. This exciting value proposition has seen the LKYGBPC grow in reach and impact, with the 10th edition attracting entries from 650 universities across 60 countries.

The LKYGBPC mirrors the development of Singapore's start-up ecosystem, which has blossomed from its modest start into a vibrant landscape of start-ups and venture capitalists today. Platforms like the

LKYGBPC serve as a launch pad for start-ups to raise money, participate in prestigious accelerators, and grow our ecosystem.

Entrepreneurship is not merely measured by business outcomes. The LKYGBPC offers an invaluable journey, through mentoring, networking sessions, and pitching opportunities. The networks and communities formed through the LKYGBPC spark new waves of innovation and collaboration across boundaries.

Every start-up journey is different, but common across them are the qualities of perseverance, conviction, and resourcefulness. Through the stories and experiences of the nine finalists of the 10th edition of the LKYGBPC, this book offers an intimate perspective on the start-up journey, and the quest to Reimagine Smart, Sustainable, and Resilient Cities, one start-up at a time. I hope this will inspire more young people to bravely venture forth and pursue their entrepreneurial aspirations.

My heartiest congratulations to the Singapore Management University's Institute of Innovation and Entrepreneurship for nurturing successive generations of young entrepreneurs and start-ups, in Singapore, ASEAN, and across the world. I wish you continued success in mobilizing young people, investors, and companies to uncover new opportunities and solutions, and build a better world.

Heng Swee Keat
Deputy Prime Minister and Coordinating
Minister for Economic Policies
Singapore

About the Lee Kuan Yew Global Business Plan Competition (LKYGBPC)

The Lee Kuan Yew Global Business Plan Competition (LKYGBPC) is a biennial university start-up challenge in Singapore, which is organized by the Institute of Innovation and Entrepreneurship (IIE) at Singapore Management University. The LKYGBPC derives its name from Singapore's founding Prime Minister Lee Kuan Yew who developed the country's defining business plan, bringing Singapore onto the global stage. It is this spirit of entrepreneurship, innovation, and ambition that the competition enshrines.

About the Authors

 **Chiraphol N Chiyachantana** is an Assistant Professor of Finance (Education) at Singapore Management University. His teaching and research interests lie primarily in Business Models and Innovation, Asset Pricing and Capital Markets, Corporate Innovations, and Sustainability. He has published his research in leading journals such as the *Journal of Finance, Journal of Financial and Quantitative Analysis, Journal of Banking and Finance, Journal of Financial Markets,* and *Journal of Financial Research.* He has won numerous teaching awards, including the Dean's Teaching Honors and the University-Wide Teaching Excellence Awards. Before joining academia, he worked as a C-level executive and board member with several listed companies in finance, education, and real estate. His experience also includes working as a consultant and conducting research workshops for Asian Development Bank, New York Stock Exchange (NYSE), U.S. Securities and Exchange Commission (SEC), Asian Development Bank (ADB), Monetary Authority of Singapore (MAS), Singapore Stock Exchange (SGX), Hong Kong Stock Exchange (HKSE), Asian Banker Association, Bank of Thailand, Security Exchange Commission of Thailand, and Stock Exchange of Thailand.

Tamas Makany is a design researcher and educator interested in how people use technology to learn, communicate, and play. Specifically, his current research focuses on conversational design, digital innovation, and entrepreneurship. He is an Associate Professor of Communication Management at Singapore Management University, Lee Kong Chian School of Business. Tamas teaches user experience, design thinking, and product innovation based on his decade-long industry experience at Silicon Valley companies such as Netflix, Microsoft, and several start-ups. He received his Ph.D. from Southampton University and was a post-doctoral visiting researcher at Stanford. Since living in Singapore, he has served the local design community by being a member of the Design Business Chamber Singapore (DBCS) and the Singapore Design Education Advisory Committee (DEAC). Tamas also mentors start-ups around the globe on how to grow their businesses and design better products through consumer insights.

David K Ding is an Associate Professor of Finance (Education) and Director of the CFA University Affiliation Program at Singapore Management University. He has more than 30 years' experience in teaching and researching at various academic institutions in Singapore and abroad. He currently teaches Finance to business and accounting undergraduates, law students, and graduate students. David's research interests lie in corporate social responsibility, sustainability, emerging financial markets, start-ups, and technopreneurship. He has written extensively and published over 100 articles in academic journals, industry outlets, books, and cases. He has received several accolades and awards for his work over the years. David is a member of the Asian Shadow Financial Regulatory Committee (a global think-tank) and is on the executive board of the Asian Finance Association, where he had previously served as president. He also serves on the editorial board of several journals, including those on sustainability.

Acknowledgments

Every two years, the campus of Singapore Management University (SMU) is buzzing with the excitement of entrepreneurs from all around the world preparing to compete in the Lee Kuan Yew Global Business Plan Competition (LKYGBPC), organized by the Institute of Innovation and Entrepreneurship (IIE) at SMU. In 2021, a year that marked the 10th edition of the competition, the buzz was mostly virtual due to the COVID-19 pandemic. However, posters were placed around the corridors and a barrage of social media campaigns called on spectators to attend the pitches of start-up founders from more than 40 countries with the latest ideas for building smart, sustainable, and resilient cities. Participants from some 650 universities, of which more than 70 were from among the world's top 100 universities, took part in the competition.

Days before the competition's finals in March 2021, the then-freshly appointed SMU faculty, Tamas Makany, stepped into the elevator on the fourth floor of the Lee Kong Chian School of Business. In the same elevator was Chiraphol New Chiyachantana. Such serendipitous meetings during the pandemic were rare when most people worked from home, so the two of them happily agreed to have lunch together. Walking toward the Canteen Bistro for a bowl of mushroom omurice, they passed by the LKYGBPC posters and started to talk about the upcoming final pitches that they planned to watch virtually on the live stream.

As New and Tamas weighed the odds of the participating teams for the grand final prizes, New remarked that all entrepreneurs and business practitioners could greatly benefit from the personal and business journeys of these exceptional founders. The lunch gave the two professors an idea — why not collect and showcase the finalists' stories in a short practitioner's book to inspire more people to pursue their entrepreneurial dreams? With Tamas's decade-long industry experience in ethnographic field research to interview people about their lives and New's expertise in business models and entrepreneurship management, the two of them grew confident that they could chronicle these stories of resilience, dedication, and resolve in the face of challenges that had come their way.

The book-writing process started and progressed over the next several months, with data collection through interviews with the founders to map their business ideas, challenges, and successes. The interviews were then crafted into narrative stories of their entrepreneurial journeys and infused with quotes, anecdotes, and market details to convey not only the successful start-up business models but also the emotions and personalities of the founders.

New and Tamas were later joined by their SMU colleague, David K Ding, who organized and structured the draft chapters into the final manuscript. David's involvement was coincidental. New and David had, in the previous year, co-authored a book on the digital transformation of businesses. New thought that David could help with repackaging the various draft chapters and contributing his insights to the book's conclusion. A meeting was later arranged with Tamas, and all three co-authors embraced the project wholeheartedly.

Just as IIE was about to launch the next competition in 2023, it is our profound pleasure to present this book that celebrates some of the entrepreneurial successes of the 10th edition of the LKYGBPC. We hope to inspire many current and future start-up founders to chase their dreams and experiment with business models that can bring about the next round of winners in this or future editions of the LKYGBPC.

This book would not have been possible without the collective efforts of numerous individuals. The authors' deepest gratitude goes to the founders participating in the 10th LKYGBPC. This book is about them and their inspiring journeys. In particular, we thank Atif Syed (Wootzano), Or Litman (Eyelight), Xiaojun Yan (Cytoniche), Jonathan Ng (Iterative Scopes), Siddharth Jadhav (Polybee), Justin Liu and Met Li (Zhen Robotics), Hongjie Liu and Xiaofeng Yang (Reexen), Pham Hong Van (Emmay), and Dr. Maarit Kahila and Dr. Anna Broberg (Maptionnaire) for opening up and sharing their personal journey with us, and for allowing us to write about them for the benefit of others after them.

We are incredibly grateful to the organizer of the 10th LKYGBPC, the Institute of Innovation and Entrepreneurship (IIE) at Singapore Management University for giving us the opportunity to connect with the start-ups and for helping us collect the stories, pitch decks, and background materials of the competition finalists. We especially thank the Director, Koh Foo Hau, for penning the introductory chapter, and Shirley Wong, Entrepreneur-in-Residence at SMU's IIE and Managing Partner at TNF Ventures Pte. Ltd., for her guidance in the final touches of the book. We are appreciative of the collaboration and endless resources provided by IIE. The following team members deserve special mention: Susan Tan, June Seah, Amelia Chen, Emelynn Siah, Wei Jing Ng, and Christine Wee.

We are humbled by the inspiring Foreword written by Singapore's Deputy Prime Minister, Mr. Heng Swee Keat, and the supportive endorsements by our reviewers Professor Erkko Autio, Professor in Technology Venturing and Entrepreneurship at Imperial College Business School, and Professor Brian Janz, Professor of Management Information Systems at The University of Memphis, who provided generous comments, constructive feedback, and strong encouragement.

We are highly grateful to Hao Liang, Co-Director at Singapore Green Finance Centre, and our colleagues and staff at SMU, who encouraged and enabled us to write this book. Our wonderful research assistants — Natalie Khoo, Zhong Min Goh, Sharlene Yeo, Katrina Gor, and Ellis Noval — were unrelenting in their support to help us identify and make sense of the initial materials provided to us. We hope this project has given them valuable insights into the process of research and that it will contribute to their future success.

We thank Karen Schwartz and Alfred Siew for their help with the early drafts of the book. Thaheera Althaf, our initial editor at World Scientific Publishing, followed by Kura Sunaina, helped us navigate the complexities of book-writing and guided us toward the completion of the book — we are truly grateful for their team's patience and professionalism. We are also thankful to Nimal Koliyat of World Scientific Publishing, who served as our project manager.

Last, but not least, we would like to express our heartfelt gratitude to our dear friends and family for their unwavering support and enthusiasm throughout the creation of this book. Your belief in us and patience with us while we dedicated ourselves to writing mean the world to us. We hope that after reading these inspiring stories, you understand (and forgive) our relentless enthusiasm for working on this project.

Contents

From Vision to Reality: A Selection of Success Stories from the Lee Kuan Yew Global Business Plan Competition

We live in tumultuous times — climate change, recurring public health crises, and threats to food security are just some of the problems that have grown in scale and complexity in an interconnected era. Countries and regions worldwide have been pouring increased funding into Research and Development (R&D) to bolster their resilience against these global challenges. Yet, combating such challenges requires more than just resilience — the R&D undertaken to address the underlying issues can potentially unlock growth opportunities through entrepreneurial activities. Some examples include Moderna, Tesla, and Impossible Food, all of which are billion-dollar companies led by visionary entrepreneurs who have developed valuable products to tackle thorny global issues.

As defined by Schumpeter (1934), an entrepreneur is a person who utilizes new information to transform existing goods, create higher-quality goods, employ innovative methods of production, access new markets, tap into new sources of supply, and/or organize industry differently.

By linking inventions and resources, entrepreneurs generate wealth and produce noteworthy economic and social changes.

Answering Singapore's Call for Innovation: The Lee Kuan Yew Global Business Plan Competition

Few are born entrepreneurs, and not many will succeed. To succeed as an entrepreneur, one has to have some extraordinary qualities such as high energy levels, a cut of mind that sees opportunities where others see problems, and a keen sense of what product or service will be profitable.

— **Lee Kuan Yew**, Senior Minister, 2002

The late Mr. Lee Kuan Yew expounded at length during his inaugural speech at the Ho Rih Hwa Leadership in Asia Public Lecture at Singapore Management University (SMU) that entrepreneurs are a rare breed. He recognized the importance of entrepreneurship in driving innovation and dynamism in a small and open economy such as Singapore. It epitomizes the qualities — creativity and perseverance — that allow Singapore, being but a little red dot on the globe, to enjoy a position that belies its size. As such, the always visionary former Senior Minister agreed to lend his name to create the Lee Kuan Yew Global Business Plan Competition to turbo-charge the growth of the entrepreneurship ecosystem in Singapore.

The biennial university start-up challenge — the Lee Kuan Yew Global Business Plan Competition (LKYGBPC) — which answers the call for innovation, was the first of its kind to encourage university students in Singapore and around the world to solve the world's problems through entrepreneurship.

The LKYGBPC is organized by the Institute of Innovation and Entrepreneurship (IIE) at Singapore Management University. It derived its name from Singapore's founding Prime Minister, who developed the country's defining business plan in bringing Singapore onto the global stage. It is this spirit of entrepreneurship, innovation, and ambition that the competition enshrines.

Themed "Reimagine Smart, Sustainable & Resilient Cities," the 10th edition of the LKYGBPC brought together the brightest minds from among the world's most entrepreneurial universities to address the challenges of the 21st century and reimagine a smart, sustainable, and resilient future. Among the approximately 650 global universities that participated in the competition are more than 70 of the world's top 100 universities, including Harvard, MIT, Oxford, Stanford, and Tsinghua universities.

Over the five-day competition held in Singapore, there were more than 28,000 event attendees (physical and virtual), with the participants vying for prizes valued at more than USD1.5 million.

Ideas as Coalition Magnets to Effect Change

Be it the application of AI to empower doctors with real-time computer-aided detection and diagnostic tools, facilitation of pollination through autonomous drones to enhance global food security, or the use of 3D microtissue engineering technology in large-scale manufacturing of high-quality stem cells, student entrepreneurs who participated in the LKYGBPC are part of the select few who successfully tapped into innovations discovered in universities to change the way people around the world live, work, and play.

It's not just the innovativeness of their ideas but the imagination and the impact of their ideas globally that have caught our attention.

— **Nicholas Nash**, Co-Founder of Asia Partners
(Judge for 10th edition of LKYGBPC)

These start-up founders not only impressed the judges but their ability to precisely identify problems, design solutions backed by innovative technologies, and share their vision imbues the power to impact change as they build coalitions that influence resource allocation. Due to the fresh perspectives that each of these entrepreneurs bring to solving problems, they can bring together stakeholders with decision-making authority — be it customers, partners, or investors — to reimagine the future going forward.

This observation is reflected in their revenues and the funds raised by the alumni of the LKYGBPC. Several of the past participants are on track to hitting millions in sales — in April 2021, Wootzano signed contracts worth over USD350 million, while Reexen is expecting orders valued at over USD40 million in 2022. Collectively, the finalists of the LKYGBPC have raised more than USD845 million in the five years since 2017, demonstrating the role entrepreneurs play in influencing resource allocation toward solving world problems.

This book details the entrepreneurial journey of each start-up founder — from cradle to success. By reflecting on their personal stories, we provide aspiring entrepreneurs with potential roadmaps on how they, too, can discover market opportunities, organize resources, and achieve success. We also share the challenges the founders faced and how they overcame the seemingly insurmountable odds.

The Ideas of Successful Entrepreneurs

Everyone faces problems, but what provides entrepreneurs with inspiration and motivation for that viable solution? According to Djankov *et al.* (2006), the social environment plays an important role.

Or Litman, co-founder of EyeLight, watched her grandfather suffer from complications of diabetes, causing him to lose his eyesight over time.

This motivated her to develop a 3D solution that helps blind or partially sighted individuals better navigate their surroundings and to immerse in entertainment and e-commerce.

Pham Hong Van, the founder of Emmay, saw how her family managed to lift themselves out of financial hardship by selling mushroom floss and other mushroom-based products. Seeing the burgeoning demand in this area, Pham was inspired to create alternative plant-based instant foods.

Jonathan Ng, the co-founder of Iterative Scopes, was on a trip to the post-Khmer Rouge regime in Cambodia when his eyes were opened to the gaps in healthcare in the country, inspiring him to work on healthcare innovations.

Aside from their social environment, work experience is yet another important source for generating new ideas (Shane, 2000; Politis, 2005; Shepherd and DeTienne, 2005). Work experience exposes individuals to unique customer insights such as problems, viable markets, product availability, and competitive resources that enhance their ability to identify shortcomings or inefficiencies in business policies or operations. More actionable insights can also trigger ideas for new or better ways of serving customers and markets that connect to unmet needs for which consumers and firms are willing to pay.

Given that the LKYGBPC is a university-based start-up challenge, it is not surprising that most business ideas in the competition were generated when the student founders were developing their Ph.D. theses.

Reexen's co-founder Dr. Hongjie Liu was working on an analog circuit design for her Ph.D. thesis when she saw a need to develop low-power energy-efficient integrated chips for the Internet of Things (IoT) sensors used in AR/VR/XR, autonomous driving, and other smart wearable devices.

CytoNiche's co-founders Dr. Xiaojun Yan, Dr. Wei Liu, and Professor Yanan Du discovered a market opportunity to consistently supply large numbers of stem cells while developing the ideas for their theses on 3D microtissue engineering.

After realizing how saturated the market for medical robotics is, the founder of Wootzano, Dr. Atif Syed, leveraged the robotics technology he developed while working on his Ph.D. thesis and applied it to an alternative industry — agricultural robotics — to reduce the manpower required for fruit-picking.

Dr. Maarit Kahila and Dr. Anna Broberg, co-founders of Maptionnaire, juggled between completing their Ph.D. theses and running their company, an urban planning platform that streamlines the community engagement process, facilitating collaboration between urban planners and their citizens.

Yet others found it worth their while to abandon the pursuit of their Ph.D. degree dream in exchange for something they deem to be infinitely more valuable — the development of an exciting new start-up. It's now or never!

Siddharth Jadhav, the founder of Polybee, gave up on his ambition of pursuing a Ph.D. in aerodynamics when he chanced, by accident, upon the idea of agricultural innovation by developing "smart" mechanical bees to pollinate crops that improves food security for the vulnerable.

Justin Liu of ZhenRobotics withdrew from his Ph.D. studies in computer science to engage in a robotics and artificial intelligence project. Justin's start-up company develops service robots that revolutionize last-mile delivery, mobile security patrol, and unmanned robotic cleaning.

There are many sources of start-up ideas outside of the university environment. Still, it is no coincidence that many successful ventures originated from universities since research programs and the free-spirited environment within universities are usually fertile ground for innovation and entrepreneurship.

Grit Differentiates Successful Entrepreneurs from the Rest

Success is not imminent even with a brilliant idea. For every successful start-up featured in this book, thousands more with a similar idea would never see the light of day.

Failure is part of the process, and it is likely that the first idea would not work out the way one imagined. However, it is crucial to keep going instead of giving up.
— **Justin Liu**, Founder of ZhenRobotics

From market validation and funding to building a high-performance team and a sustainable business model, 101 things could go wrong. The single most important quality that differentiates successful start-up founders from others is grit. How does one separate the "wheat" from the "chaff ?" In a study by Mooradian *et al.* (2016), perseverance of effort is found to be significantly and positively correlated to innovation success, which contributes to increasing company performance.

There were many difficulties on the way to founding EyeLight. Potential investors found the idea exciting, but thought the market was too small to invest in. The main thing that helped me through was my passion and the support from my friends and family.
— **Or Litman**, Co-Founder of EyeLight

It can be emotionally draining for entrepreneurs to receive negative feedback, but those student founders who embraced the feedback and continually honed their propositions are those who eventually made the exponential leap and achieved success. In the meantime, having a supportive network through mentors, entrepreneurial friends, and family is equally important to lend the necessary support for building resilience.

Drivers of Success
Receptiveness to Feedback

Beyond emotional resilience, what steps can entrepreneurs take to make that exponential leap? Talk to any student founders, and they will tell you the importance of getting as much information about your idea and its industry as possible.

Empirical evidence has revealed a strong correlation between prior knowledge and the discovery of opportunities (Ucbasaran *et al.*, 2008), firm growth (Cooper *et al.*, 1994), and overall venture success (Romanelli, 1989). In fact, the lack of domain-specific knowledge has been shown to predict business failure (Ucbasaran *et al.*, 2008; Shepherd, 2003; Song *et al.*, 2008). How, then, can one garner sufficient knowledge about the business idea? Talking to others about your idea is one of the best ways to do so.

I think when you get an idea and you think it's interesting, you can already start to meet people and then verify whether it's great or not. And, mostly, don't listen to 90% of the people. Only listen to the 10% of wise people.
— **Dr. Hongjie Liu**, Founder and CEO of Reexen

Given the higher levels of uncertainty within the environment in which entrepreneurs work, it is very important to talk to stakeholders and get feedback to reduce potential blind spots and, hence, the unsystematic risk of undertaking a venture. Not all feedback lends an equal amount of weight. Howell (2021) finds that only private feedback from experts leads to an improvement in resource allocation and efficiency of innovation.

Metacognitive Ability

The level of metacognition, or thinking about thinking, for entrepreneurs also plays a part. Entrepreneurs with high metacognitive knowledge can use feedback more effectively than founders with lower metacognitive knowledge to achieve higher performance (Haynie *et al.*, 2012).

Partnerships

Even if the business idea is executed brilliantly in one market, several difficulties can confront technology entrepreneurs as they expand their operations. The venture must undertake aggressive investments — in areas such as marketing or manufacturing — to simultaneously persuade customers of their novel value proposition, manage multiple dimensions of uncertainty, and focus scarce organizational resources while avoiding "detection" and aggressive response by established players (Gans and Stern, 2003). In other words, this implies that forming strategic partnerships is paramount to continued growth.

Since start-ups tend to lack the resources required to leverage short-lived proprietary advantages, cooperation with larger partners, whether upstream or downstream, is increasingly seen as imperative in helping them achieve global-scale efficiencies and withstand new competition (Wright and Dana, 2003).

> *I learned that, in a successful business, the priority is about constantly maintaining your relationships with your stakeholders, employees, and partners.*
> — **Justin Liu**, Founder of ZhenRobotics

As Justin Liu of ZhenRobotics has shared, cultivating strong partnerships with e-commerce giants, commercial companies, and hospitals is how his company developed many robotic products with a strong product–market fit quickly, allowing it to expand within a short time.

Jonathan Ng of Iterative Scopes, too, credits his strong partnerships with companies such as Provation Medical in quickly developing and delivering products to the market, providing the necessary impetus to raise more than USD150 million in funding.

Not only are corporate partnerships useful but the ability of start-ups to leverage assistance from governmental and non-profit organizations can provide the necessary resources to kick-start and grow their enterprises. The founders of CytoNiche, for example, shared about how the Technology Transfer Office at Tsinghua University connected them with the relevant government ministries such as the Zhongguancun (ZGC) for funding, allowing them to launch two clinical trials in 2021. CytoNiche managed to secure more than 60 patents, including 30 granted patents, three Patent Cooperation Treaty (PCT) patents, and eight international patents under filing, at the time of writing, to enhance its market value and gain a competitive edge. It is no wonder that CytoNiche won more than 100 customers, 10 distributors, and 50% of the mesenchymal stem cell therapy companies that have filed an Investigational New Drug (IND) application in China under its portfolio, achieving more than a 500% increase in sales in 2021.

Polybee founder Siddharth Jadhav detailed how Temasek Foundation, a non-profit organization under the philanthropic arm of Singapore's state sovereign fund Temasek Holdings, went above and beyond to de-risk his venture by providing the initial grant to enable resource-constrained entrepreneurs like him to develop a viable product full time.

Beyond reiterating the feedback and execution of start-up entrepreneurs, the ability of the founder team to seek collaborations with the right partners is increasingly seen as a critical success factor for the start-ups of tomorrow.

Illuminating the Road to a Brighter Future

In the subsequent chapters, you will read about the stories of nine university start-ups that have emerged as finalists in the Lee Kuan Yew Global Business Plan Competition. They originate from around the world and have employed diverse business models with ideas spanning robotics, biosciences, food security, agriculture, and manufacturing. The common thread among these start-ups is that they all possess grit, metacognition, and receptiveness to feedback. They also possess the ability to form coalitions of support that have enabled them to realize the vision of their future — the very qualities that Singapore's founding father, the late Mr. Lee Kuan Yew, embodied as he led Singapore to independence and laid the foundations that put the island city-state onto the world map.

As we celebrate the trailblazing spirit embodied in changemakers, the Lee Kuan Yew Global Business Plan Competition galvanizes entrepreneurs worldwide to reimagine a smarter, more sustainable, and more resilient future.

CHAPTER 2

Wootzano: Dexterous Fruit-Picking Robots

Wootzano is an England-based robotics company focused on the agricultural industry. It uses machine learning to automate fruit and vegetable sorting, packing, and labeling. The company aims to produce robotic systems that can sense and feel like human workers. As an example, the company had built a proprietary hand-gripper covered with WootZkin, the company's electronic skin, to do the work of three humans in a day.

Chairman, CEO, and founder of Wootzano, Dr. Atif Syed, recalls first hearing about the challenge of tomato-picking in 2016 while attending an executive committee meeting of the UK's Institution of Engineering and Technology (IET) on robotics, where he served as the youngest-ever elected board member. A fellow committee member pointed out that if only robots had the required dexterity and computer vision, they would be ideally positioned for fruit-picking. The possibility immediately sparked Dr. Syed's interest as he thought about how to position robots to address the issue. "Robots are ideally suited for this repetitive task. They wouldn't get bored of it and could work 24/7," he concluded.

In August 2016, Dr. Syed, who holds a Ph.D. in engineering and bio-nanotechnology, completed his doctoral thesis and, within a year, founded Wootzano. He soon discovered its robots could transform the fruit-picking process. To successfully navigate fruit-picking, it is important to ensure the soft, delicate produce doesn't get damaged or bruised on its journey from the vine to the supermarket shelves.

How do you manipulate this? That was a challenge, and that's something we were able to solve. We were able to solve it with the electronic skin we had. So, we started working towards developing the prototype.

— **Dr. Atif Syed**, Founder and CEO, Wootzano

It took about a year of prototyping to increase the production of these advanced sensors from a few sensors a week to just over 180 a day at launch. "We're doing a lot more than that now," he adds confidently.

Initially, he had intended to build bioengineering solutions to help treat cancer. As an undergraduate student, he was interested in new ways to deliver cancer drugs into the human body, using flexible polymers integrated with nanoparticles. "I got really fascinated by nanotechnology and the ability to engineer very small machines and effectively make a macro or massive impact by using these little machines — that was very exciting," he says. In 2013, without an inclination to become an academic, he enrolled in the Engineering, Electronics, and Bionanotechnology Ph.D. program at the University of Edinburgh. He researched ways to equip robots with polymers to act as a form of robotic skin equipped with heat and pressure sensors. "This was a new feature that robots didn't have at the time."

However, Dr. Syed quickly realized that he would have to find a new application for his technology, as the barriers to entry into the medical robotics field were high, and the returns were uncertain. The IET meeting in 2016 was a critical turning point for Dr. Syed and came at just the right moment. It presented a problem that needed a solution in an arena that interested him greatly.

Problem and Opportunity: Serving a Need

It's really replicating what a human is doing and going beyond that.
— **Dr. Atif Syed**, Founder and CEO, Wootzano

Tomato-picking is tough manual work. It requires dexterity and hours of long, repetitive labor. The pay is low, and the labor turnover high, with fruit pickers leaving almost daily. Fruit packing companies struggle to find and retain manual laborers, who need to be trained to the standards required by the industry. Fruit packers must also follow tight requirements set forth by retailers, and pickers must be educated to guarantee that the quality of products is maintained. As a result, the typical profit margin resulting from using manual fruit packers is only 1–4%. However, technology can change that. With the addition of more machinery during the COVID-19 pandemic alone, margins are up to some 6.5%. And that's only the beginning of a problem that has long needed a solution.

Additionally, global conditions such as Brexit and COVID-19 have shifted the worker demographics and access to labor. New laws, restrictions, and lockdowns have strained the picking process and shown points of weakness in the supply chain that need to be addressed. Otherwise, the fruit will be discarded or not reach its intended consumers because there aren't enough people available to pick it.

The timing was right for the application of a sophisticated AI technology, Dr. Syed explains, and the problem and solution were a clear match. As an entrepreneur, Dr. Syed believes in building technology to address real-world problems. That means there must be a commercial need, or its perceived — or actual — utility could fall flat. "You should then go and see what the pain point is and how the technology you've developed can solve it, as opposed to …, let's build it, basically finish the whole product, and then take it out and market it," he explains. So, it's essential to ensure the issue is real and the need is clear.

Learning about the needs of fruit packers gave him an insight into the industry and a vision for applying his technology. He saw a robust market and a unique opportunity for using robots sensitive enough to handle dexterous tasks, such as delicate fruit-picking and packaging. The need for a new fruit-picking solution opened a new door for putting his robotics and nanotechnology expertise to work. Moreover, it offered a meaningful application and unique business opportunity in agricultural robotics that would employ his robots to solve a significant problem. The result would impact not just farmers and the companies that distributed their produce but also entire supply chains and end consumers. "This was the great pivot we made … to agricultural robotics. And I am very happy that we did this," he says.

The robots' dexterity offered a desirable possibility for revolutionizing the market. Meanwhile, the options already in the market were too costly for customers, who could not commit to a large CapEx upfront as any equipment, asset, or capital expenditure needed to show returns in the short term. "They need to make sure they get their money back within three years or less," he says.

He sought to make not just robots but also robots priced at a point that would resonate with customers. The robotic system is priced in such a way that the customer gets a rapid return on their investment. "Our customers get their money back within 12 months, at the very least," he explains.

Solution

This was a new feature robots didn't have at the time.
— **Dr. Atif Syed**, Founder and CEO, Wootzano

In a scientific park in Sedgefield, a Northeast English town surrounded by gently sloping fields, Dr. Syed is deeply immersed in innovating advanced robots to help tackle this agricultural challenge. He has built a process and developed a technology that can transform how tomatoes and other fruits are picked. Wootzano's robotic skin, using proprietary AI technology, can now evaluate data such as pressure, firmness, temperature, humidity, and chemical signals with more precision than human skin, explains Dr. Syed, who designed it. That gives the robots nuanced sensing abilities, efficient robotic architecture, and the ability to operate in all kinds of environments.

Wootzano uses its patented electronic skin, proprietary hardware, and machine learning algorithms to pick and package tomatoes and grapes. With fully integrated robotic packaging systems, Wootzano offers robots that can execute monotonous packaging jobs more productively and profitably than people without damaging the fresh produce. The electronic skin has been built into a robotic system with a manipulator and fingertips that can identify tomatoes, determine their ripeness, and harvest the fruit in milliseconds. The energy-efficient robots work at a constant speed and, by operating around the clock, Wootzano's customers' profit margins are expected to increase, with a one-year return on investment. In addition, robots will allow existing workers to be redeployed to more meaningful positions that are non-repetitive and less physically stressful to their health.

Robotics System — Avarai™

Jumping on this opportunity, Wootzano introduced a highly dexterous robot, Avarai™, a state-of-the-art robotics system that can work 24 hours a day, seven days a week (see Figure 1). Equipped with an electronic skin akin to human skin, it is capable of pruning, picking, and packing a wide variety of delicate and easily damaged fresh produce in a highly dexterous manner. In addition to careful handling and packing of delicate fresh

Figure 1: Avarai™, state-of-the-art robot.

produce, it can also check the quality of the produce, for example, to see how ripe it is, and determine its weight to see how much pressure to apply, so the produce isn't held too tightly in the packing process. This helps reduce food waste from improper handling or packaging. According to the company, the robots provide an exceptional return on investment (ROI) within a year. Avarai robots are expected to be in packhouses that pack more than 90% of all table grapes and 80% of vine tomatoes in the UK, supplying to all major retailers.

Each robotic system has three unique components: a patented electronic skin, a proprietary hand, and machine learning algorithms.

(1) Patented Electronic Skin — WootZkin

WootZkin is an electronic robotic skin that can be integrated into all major robotic manipulators (see Figure 2), though Wootzano prefers to have WootZkin applied only to its robotic system. It was developed using a combination of robotics and nanotechnology. In addition to being

Figure 2: WootZkin, an electronic robotic skin.

completely stretchable, bendable, and twistable, it is as soft as human skin and made from a compliant, durable material that can respond to force and pressure. This electronic skin is made up of a highly sensitive pressure sensor that is integrated with temperature and chemical sensors. Multiple functional layers add unique piezoelectric and piezoresistive responses, allowing a robot to detect pressure and slippages. The nanowires used in WootZkin are akin to mechanoreceptors (nerve endings) found on human skin. For example, an average human finger skin has 241 mechanoreceptors/ cm^2, while an average human palm skin has 58 mechanoreceptors/cm^2. WootZkin has a whopping 7,000,000,000 nanowires/cm^2, making it as sensitive as human skin, if not more.

WootZkin allows robots to handle a variety of fresh produce in a human-like manner, allowing them to become highly specialized in fresh produce packing and dexterous when executing duties. The company's patented technology equips robots with greater sensory awareness of their environments. Electronic skin enables robots to respond to how firm/soft produce is, whether it is slippery, and even estimate its temperature. Using nanostructures, the robots can use chemical analysis to "smell" the fresh produce they touch. WootZkin's Data System analyzes pressure, temperature, and chemical signatures to allow robots to manipulate items accurately and intelligently. Wootzano's robots can, as a result, trim fresh produce to the desired weights/sizes, determine freshness and shelf-life, and pack them, all in one step.

With 4G data or Wi-Fi connectivity, Wootzano's robots can constantly send usage data to its cloud network. As a result, it can advise when a skin replacement, similar to replacing an ink cartridge that is all used up, is necessary. The worn-out WootZkin may be readily peeled off and replaced with the new electronic skin. WootZkin has already scaled up technology whereby Wootzano can produce more than 384 sensors in 4 days with a 99% yield.

(2) Proprietary Hand

Wootzano's robots have an articulated six-axis arm, and its proprietary hand gripper is covered with WootZkin (see Figure 3). As a result, the work gets done effectively. Instead of existing workers risking injury from physically stressful and repetitive tasks, using the proprietary hand frees workers to be redeployed to more meaningful positions. It also allows companies to address recruitment shortages, which companies have grappled with both during the pandemic and more widely, given the work demands and low pay associated with the field. Efficient robot architecture removes these barriers to optimizing the picking process.

(3) Machine Learning Algorithms

Machine learning algorithms allow Wootzano's robots to analyze, store, and process data in a cloud network. In addition to self-learning, robots can also learn from other robots worldwide in distributed cloud networks, thereby enhancing machine learning capabilities.

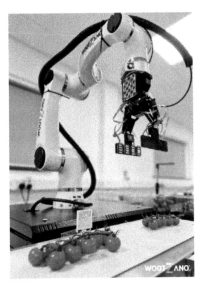

Figure 3: Wootzano's proprietary hand gripper covered with WootZkin.

Wootzano's robots use complex machine learning models to automate weight estimation, quality inspection, and even shelf-life prediction for fresh produce. Furthermore, such machine learning models help to train robots to adapt to changing environments at packaging facilities and become better and more effective at handling produce. The company continues to develop new algorithms to find more intelligent ways to pick up fresh fruit and reduce the time it takes to pick up and pack these products.

The Business Model
Target Market
Wootzano's target market comprises fruit and vegetable distributors in the United Kingdom and the EU. These wholesalers and supermarkets are important stakeholders and partners for Wootzano, especially given their significant reliance on seasonal workers and fresh produce packers to ensure they can stock their shelves and move the produce to its intended destinations.

Affirmation

Wootzano is one of the first companies in the world to mass-manufacture electronic skin and offers a fully integrated robotic system for fruits and vegetables. This has given Wootzano a significant first-to-market advantage and resulted in brand recognition among its customers. In one year, the market demand pushed Wootzano to increase its robot production from ten units a week to an average of 384 sensors in four days, with a 99% yield rate. Furthermore, Wootzano robots, electronic skin, and other technologies are entirely protected by 23 patents (as of 1st June 2022) in addition to its trade secrets, making it very difficult to copy the company. Eleven companies, representing 90% of table grapes and 80% of vine tomato fruit packers in the United Kingdom and worldwide, have expressed interest in partnering because of the robots' unique abilities.

Today, Wootzano's robots can decrease the time fresh produce spends in a supply chain, thanks to these over-the-air updates that keep performance at peak efficiency. Ultimately, fresher produce ends up on supermarket shelves rather than in neighborhood bins. Increasing productivity in the supply chain reduces overall food wastage and contributes to improving food security.

Revenue Model

Wootzano generates revenue from the initial sale of its robotic system and its monthly stream subscription fee. The monthly fee is per unit and covers the maintenance and upgrade of the robotic system, including the electric skin, which needs replacing several times a year. "As the robot learns different environments, we take that into consideration, and every couple of months, we push it back to the customer, so that's included as part of the subscription," he explains.

The back-end database includes a distributed cloud network that allows robots to learn from other robots, creating an enhanced learning environment. Additionally, Wootzano constantly upgrades its robotics system, meaning that customers can expect to receive an update every few months. With every update, the robots become more sophisticated. Since these upgrades are included in subscription fees, customers don't have to pay additional fees to have the latest performance tweaks.

These updates aim to improve performance and allow robots to become even more meaningful partners in executing these precise activities, benefiting productivity and profitability by streamlining repetitive tasks and removing inefficiencies at every level. Besides creating perpetual growth, such recurring subscription plans help Wootzano foster long-lasting connections and relationships with key stakeholders.

Insights

Dr. Syed is a trained engineer with no formal business background, although he hopes to get an MBA one day. He has built his expertise and knowledge through trial and error and uses lessons from his prior experiences to make his company the best it can be. For example, he recalls a particularly powerful incident that reinforced the importance of due diligence not only with competitors but also with investors. In 2018, he went to a group of three investors for advice and money. "When you start a business, and when you're young and excited, you go and meet people," he recalls. However, two of the investors who claimed to be able to open doors for the start-up turned out to be trouble.

Soon after signing an agreement with them, these devil investors (the opposite of the commonly known "angel" investors) began billing unapproved personal expenses and trying to put their friends in charge. One even demanded a salary equal to the amount he'd invested in the business. "We'd had enough," Dr. Syed recalls. He had to take action to save the company. "We decided to buy them off." Dr. Syed learned from this experience how critically important it is to carry out proper due diligence when investors are chosen. It can be difficult at the very early stages of the business when the founder is generally not in a strong position, but perseverance pays off in the long run. Fortunately, his investment has brought worthwhile returns, as the company's current value has meant exponential gains. It is clear the other investors missed out, he says, adding that he's grateful the misstep didn't, in the end, turn the company off its path to success. "There's a lot of learning from these events, which I'm glad happened at a time when there was not as much to lose."

Looking Ahead

Passion is important, but not enough.
> — **Dr. Atif Syed,** Founder and CEO, Wootzano

The future looks bright for Wootzano. Currently, Wootzano has nine patents under its name and is already working on orders worth more than £100 million. In April 2021, Wootzano signed a contract worth over £300 million to supply its robotic system to a large European packer that covers around 40% of the table grapes market in the UK and Europe. Reportedly one of the largest contracts signed by a British robotics manufacturer in the United Kingdom, Wootzano plans to continue to expand its reach. By 2022, Wootzano aims to penetrate the Australian, European, North American, and South African markets.

Wootzano also aims to roll out version two of its electronic skin by 2025. This improved version is expected to improve predictions on produce's freshness. More crucially, version two of its electronic skins will be tested on prosthetic limbs and robots utilized in extreme conditions, meaning it has the potential to impact industries far and wide. Backed by continued solid demands for its robotic systems, Wootzano is expected to make revenue of £39.5 million by 2024 and £275 million by 2027.

Wootzano is changing how robots connect and collaborate with humans, focusing on agricultural economics. Dr. Syed's approach is to always build solutions to scale or, as he puts it, "Be sure to reach out to the masses." In addition, he emphasizes the importance of knowing the market ahead of time. "Passion is important, but not enough. If you don't have customers, you don't have a business," he says.

CHAPTER 3

. . . .

EyeLight: Assistive Technologies for Vision Impairment

EyeLight is on a mission to use sensors to help partially sighted and blind individuals build their confidence, helping them achieve independence and ultimately promote social inclusion. The company develops technologies that help people "see" their environment through sense collaboration between hearing and touch.

The prevalence of childhood blindness is growing beyond the status of an emerging problem in the world today. It can be caused by various factors, ranging from genetically determined and congenital conditions to micronutrient deficiency (Vitamin A deficiency) and infectious conditions (measles, ophthalmia neonatorum, or rubella) to conditions requiring specialized surgical treatment such as childhood cataracts, glaucoma, and retinopathy of prematurity. EyeLight aims to improve the lives of visually impaired individuals while also altering the way blind people "see." It sets out to make sure that blind individuals can complete simple chores conveniently and easily, and that children have more opportunities to learn about objects and their environments.

Ms. Or Litman, co-founder of EyeLight Technologies, had always been an innovative and curious person, traits that would serve her well as she pursued this new endeavor. As a child, she sat with her father, peppering him with questions about how different machines worked. When she was

6 years old, she took up artistic swimming as a sport. Being the captain of her local team in Yavne, Israel, she had to develop leadership skills, such as prioritizing and handling multiple tasks. In 2010, as a high school student, Ms. Litman entered a two-year entrepreneurial program aimed at helping talented children develop leadership and entrepreneurial skills. Ms. Litman came up with the concept of EyeLight during this program. Winning the program's final competition was an early sign that she was onto something.

After a stint as a commander of a technological unit during her compulsory army service, Ms. Litman went on to study accounting. She reconnected with Omer Gohary, a trustworthy classmate she'd known since middle school. Mr. Gohary, who now held a computer science degree and an MBA in entrepreneurial studies, became EyeLight's co-founder.

Problem and Opportunity: Giving Light to the Visually Impaired

Watching her grandfather suffering from complications of diabetes that caused him to lose his eyesight over time inspired Ms. Litman to act. There weren't any existing technologies available for him to easily understand his environment at any given moment. Ms. Litman was driven to try and find a solution that would make a difference for people like her grandfather. She felt for individuals who are partially sighted or blind and the challenges they face.

> *They don't feel confident enough to be fully part of the community.*
> — **Or Litman**, Co-Founder of EyeLight Technologies

A qualified certified public accountant (CPA) with training in accounting and statistics, Ms. Litman didn't have a medical background or formal business experience. Still, she was passionate about helping provide a resource for individuals with sight limitations.

Lack of Assistive Tools: The world has not yet addressed in sufficient ways the needs of people with sight limitations. Guide sticks and guide dogs remain the most common assistive tools for the partially sighted and blind to navigate their everyday surroundings. However, these are not sufficiently intuitive to help the visually impaired achieve independence in daily activities. While guide sticks and guide dogs can help individuals with indoor and outdoor navigation, they cannot guide them in activities such as eating, drinking, shopping, or locating an item's whereabouts. Meanwhile, restaurants in the US, Europe, and the Asia-Pacific offer "Dining in the Dark" meal experiences that give diners a sense of what the partially sighted and blind face in their daily lives.

Solution

The need to navigate different settings with limited vision proved to be a very real problem with a very tangible solution. Presenting the case, the team managed to secure a non-equity investment from an Israeli social incubator program in 2019 — and EyeLight was born. The company was originally called BlindTech, but changed its name early on to EyeLight, a play on the Hebrew words for "light" and the person who can see light.

Fundamentally, EyeLight's technology guides users through their surroundings by facilitating the transfer of information between other senses. A 3D wearable camera captures the surroundings in real time and the technology analyzes the surroundings to deliver vocal and tactile outputs to the user. The user gets information on traffic lights and the surfaces around them, all delivered via a Bluetooth® earpiece.

Aimed at helping individuals achieve independence while navigating their urban surroundings, EyeLight hopes to use hearing and touch to compensate for the visual gap. With the help of highly advanced algorithms and technologies such as 3D mapping, image processing, machine learning, and computerized artificial intelligence (AI) simulation, EyeLight provides high-resolution sensory information customized to individual user needs. This is done through EyeLight's very own revolutionary wearable product for the partially sighted and blind.

3D Real-Time Product: EyeLight's 3D real-time product (see Figure 1) is revolutionary and comes with a wearable camera, tactile surface, and smartphones. These items allow users to substitute the sense of sight through hearing and touch. In a cognitive experiment of the demo product with 20 participants, 83% had navigated more efficiently and more quickly.

The product includes the following (see Figure 2):

(1) **Wearable Camera**: A wearable camera in an eyeglass captures the surroundings in real time and transfers these inputs into EyeLight's analytical system.

(2) **3D Tactile Surface**: As the real-time inputs are captured and analyzed, a 3D tactile surface output is formed. This helps to model the

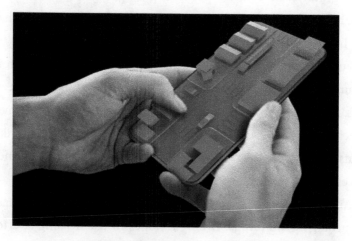

Figure 1: EyeLight's 3D real-time product.

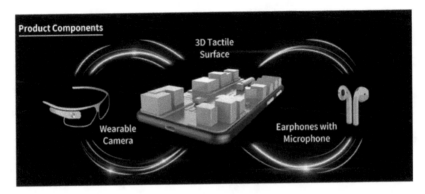

Figure 2: EyeLight's product components.

surrounding environment, enabling users to touch and feel the situation around them.

(3) **Earphones with Microphone**: Bluetooth® earphones and a microphone are used to disseminate instructions and information to users. Through the Bluetooth® earphones, users can receive details on traffic light signals as well as GPS directions and other valuable information.

EyeLight also allows partially sighted or blind individuals to fully immerse themselves in entertainment and e-commerce. There are two ways in which EyeLight hopes its 3D real-time product can help the partially sighted and blind build up their confidence to be independent:

(1) **Spatial Awareness and Indoor and Outdoor Navigation**: Spatial awareness refers to one's ability to recognize their environment and interact with their surroundings. Being partially sighted or blind can affect one's spatial perception of their body and environment, making it difficult to interpret and navigate their surroundings. EyeLight's 3D real-time product helps individuals distinguish left from right, avoid obstacles, and locate an item's whereabouts for easier grabbing.

This, in turn, builds spatial awareness and encourages better navigation skills, which are necessary for achieving independence.

(2) **Entertainment and E-Commerce**: Traditionally, partially sighted and blind individuals have not had the privilege of enjoying entertainment or e-commerce activities. Being partially sighted or blind affects one's entire experience, making it difficult to make purchases online. EyeLight's 3D real-time product can turn pictures into 3D tangible models that are more realistic and detailed than pictures and sounds alone. This, in turn, transforms the customer's experience and allows individuals to enjoy the full entertainment and e-commerce experience in ways that would have been otherwise inaccessible.

EyeLight's assistive technologies replace the sense of sight through hearing and touch such that individuals can feel and navigate through complex environments in an equanimous manner. Besides, partially sighted and blind individuals can now fully immerse themselves in the entertainment and e-commerce experience. More importantly, it builds up their confidence to be independent.

Business Model

Target Market

Health organizations, insurance companies, and commercial businesses targeting individuals suffering from moderate to severe vision impairment or blindness are important stakeholders and partners. Millions of people stand to benefit from EyeLight. In 2020, 338 million persons globally were estimated to be visually impaired. Of these, 295 million had moderate to severe vision impairment, and 43 million were blind.[1] These numbers do

---

[1] https://www.iapb.org/learn/vision-atlas/magnitude-and-projections/.

not consider the fact that 1.1 billion people live with functional presbyopia, a type of vision loss. Moreover, world blindness and visual impairment numbers are expected to continue to rise (see Figure 3).

Affirmation

EyeLight possesses a first-mover advantage in the market as one of the first companies in the world to produce assistive technology products to help improve the lives of people with vision disabilities. In fact, 90% of the participants who took part in EyeLight's cognitive experiment of the demo product reported that they would use the 3D real-time product routinely.

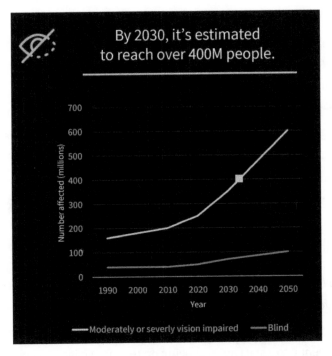

Figure 3: Estimated market size from 1990 to 2050.

Revenue Model

Revenue at EyeLight comes from two sources — a one-time sale of the 3D real-time product and a premium charged for add-on services. Examples of premium services include 3D FaceTime features, long-distance views, and customized recommendations for the full customer experience on entertainment and e-commerce sites.

Insights

Founding EyeLight was not without its challenges. For example, potential investors found the idea exciting, but thought the market was too small to invest in. Additionally, they questioned whether EyeLight could deliver on its product promises. "The main thing that helped me through tough times was my passion about the topic and the support from my friends and family," says Ms. Litman. She had to be nimble and manage constantly changing expectations and challenges, as well as be prepared to hear "no" many times. Hearing "no" was emotionally draining — but Litman did not give up. Rather, she says, staying optimistic was a key to her success. She was driven by her mission, her conviction, and her determination to succeed. "But ultimately you only need one 'yes' so you keep on calling and emailing," she says. "You need to believe in your idea, no matter how long it takes for others to also believe in you."

Critical Milestones

Letting go of the third co-founder at the beginning was a pivotal moment as it cemented the direction and values of the company. Building a team is fundamental to a start-up and being on the same page is crucial. Of her remaining co-founder, Omer Gohary, Ms. Litman says, "Omer really understands me. He sees me for who I am as a person."

More than building a strong team, Ms. Litman revealed that another key factor was the strength of their network. "Relevant connections and network are the most important assets we gained," she explains.

Israel is affectionately known as the "Start-up Nation" for its dynamic ecosystem for entrepreneurs. However, as EyeLight is focused on hardware, not software or IoT, finding resources and relevant connections proved challenging. For example, the company got an invitation to attend one of the largest computer and technology trade shows in the world, called COMPUTEX, in Taipei, Taiwan, in 2019. "When we went there, there were so many companies and investors interested in what we do, much more than in Israel," says Ms. Litman.

Fortunately, investors in Israel had already provided both the financial and technological support that allowed EyeLight to further develop its technology. EyeLight's initial funding came from NESS in Israel that gave the company a subsidy for a two-year program to develop its entrepreneurial skills and for technical support.[2]

Looking Ahead

In 2016, the assistive technologies for the partially sighted industry were worth USD3.4 billion and, by 2026, it is expected to achieve a valuation of USD7.1 billion. This is an impressive compounded annual growth rate (CAGR) of 8.5% from 2018 to 2026 (see Figure 4). With EyeLight having the first-mover advantage in 3D real-time products, it is well positioned to capture such growth in the market.

---

[2] https://www.ness-tech.co.il/. NESS is a very well-known and popular program in Israel for tech start-ups.

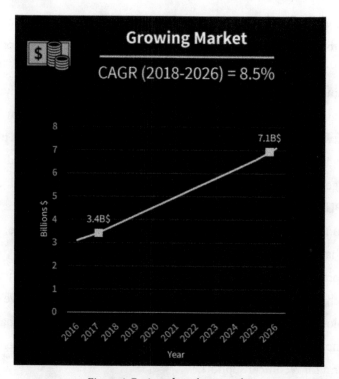

Figure 4: Projected market growth.

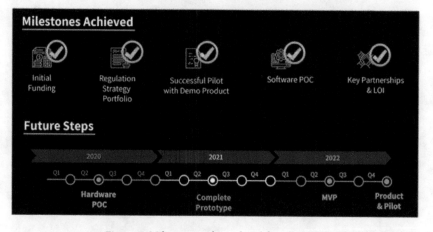

Figure 5: Milestones achieved and future plans.

With funding secured, a successful pilot launch of its demo product, proof of concept completed for its software and technology, and various key partnerships signed, the future looks bright for EyeLight (see Figure 5).

Primarily focused within the medical technology and sight sensor industry, EyeLight is reshaping and improving the quality of life for people with visual disabilities. Within three years, EyeLight has already successfully impacted partially sighted and blind individuals by helping to build their confidence, helping them achieve independence, and ultimately promoting social inclusion.

CHAPTER 4

CytoNiche: Experts in Mass Manufacturing of 3D Live Cells

When she completed her chemical and biomolecular engineering undergraduate studies at the National University of Singapore in 2012, Dr. Xiaojun Yan had two choices: follow many of her classmates into the commercial sector or keep honing her expertise through more research before striking out on her own as an entrepreneur.

For the Singaporean, the path ahead was clear. She chose to continue in academia to complete her doctoral studies with the caveat that she would one day transform the ideas and expertise from her research into a commercial opportunity to benefit society. Thus began a six-year biomedical engineering Ph.D. program at Tsinghua University in Beijing, backed by a full government scholarship.

This was a perfect match because Dr. Yan had been looking for a country with a robust business environment and a fast-growing market that could take up her technology. It was only a few years after the Beijing Olympic Games, and she saw that the bio-technology industry was growing rapidly in China.

The university was also where she met her two eventual co-founders of CytoNiche, a Beijing-based biotech start-up specializing in stem cell production. In August 2018, the company was established by Dr. Yan, her laboratory colleague, Dr. Wei Liu, and their Ph.D. supervisor, Professor Yanan Du.

The basis of the company came from the two students' Ph.D. theses on microtissue engineering for stem cell production. Today, CytoNiche is on a journey to offer affordable solutions for the large-scale manufacturing of high-quality cells through its 3D microtissue engineering technology.

Problem and Opportunity: Filling the Need for High-Quality Stem Cells

Large-scale, live-cell manufacturing has become a growing concern for biotechnology and pharmaceutical companies, which require many high-quality cells to support effective cell and gene therapy, which is the next-generation medical technology.

However, when the founders of CytoNiche conducted a thorough market analysis and talked to potential investors, they realized that the real need was not about applying stem cell drugs but how they were made.

> *Even today, there are a lot of stem cell drugs under development.*
> *These companies all focus on the downstream to develop the*
> *therapy itself. What we saw was that nobody was focusing on the*
> *upstream, which is the production process.*
> — **Dr. Xiaojun Yan**, Co-Founder and CTO

Increased Demand for Live Cells

With the development of science and technology in recent years, the use of live cells has expanded, and companies now require greater amounts of live cells for various uses (see Figure 1). Traditionally, live cells can only be used to produce vaccines, antibodies, or proteins. Today, live cells can be used as final products, and there are 14 cellular drugs approved worldwide thus far. Other live cell advancements include regenerative

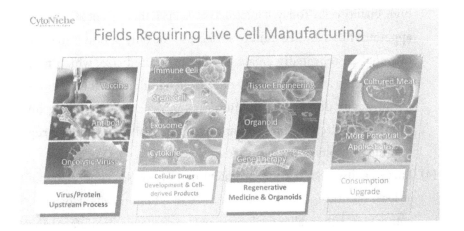

Figure 1: Demand for live cells.

medicines such as stem cell therapy and bioartificial liver and producing clean meat. However, as the benefits and purpose of live cells amplify, the supply struggles to keep up with industry demand due to the complexity surrounding live-cell production.

Four main reasons contribute to this bottleneck:

(1) **Intensive Labor**: It takes ten workers 40 days working continuously to produce one billion cells using traditional 2D cell culture flasks. Every one billion cells produced can only treat one patient suffering from graft-versus-host disease (GVHD), construct half a bioartificial liver, or produce 10g of meat. Live-cell manufacturing is not only labor-intensive but also costly and time-consuming.

(2) **Limited Capacity**: As with every production facility, there is always a limit in capacity when it comes to allowable output. Hence, manufacturing large amounts of high-quality live cells may not be sustainable for companies, given restricted production capabilities and inefficiencies.

(3) **Batch Variation**: Given how delicate stem cells are in nature, current biotechnology production may not be capable of producing many

high-quality cells. Today, it is hard to scale up as the current 2D culture apparatus has a limited culture surface, so the only option is to scale out, that is, repeatedly create batches of limited size, which may inadvertently affect the quality of cells. In addition, batch variations could occur during the manufacturing process depending on production circumstances, resulting in inconsistent cellular drug treatment results or protein/vaccine quality.

(4) **Large Facility**: For optimal production of live cells, a large facility of at least 500 m² is required to produce one billion cells. However, companies with smaller facilities may face challenges manufacturing a sizable number of live cells.

Role Delegation

In 2015, Dr. Yan and Dr. Liu thought they would create two separate but related companies where they would each act as CEO. However, they quickly realized this divided their attention too much, so they consolidated their efforts into a single company, CytoNiche.

After some deliberation, Dr. Liu became the CEO and Dr. Yan became the CTO. There were several reasons for this, including language, culture, and communication. A Singaporean with Chinese heritage, Dr. Yan was fluent in the Chinese language; however, she was not accustomed to some of the socio-cultural rules of running a business in China.

"In China, you need to drink and be loud while doing business with others," she said, adding that she was more of an introvert and interested in building more profound technological expertise. "Being a CTO suits me better," she explained.

As a full-time faculty member of a university, the third co-founder, Prof. Du, cannot take on a paid job; so, he serves as a scientific advisor for the company. But, all said, the three co-founders consider each other equal in all ways. "We have a harmonious way of working together," said Prof. Du.

The co-founders make decisions through a simple majority of votes. The only minor imbalance is that the CEO has more control over company matters as Dr. Liu holds slightly more shares in the company than the other two. Dr. Yan sees this as an acceptable compromise and fully trusts her business partners.

The Solution: A Better Way with CytoNiche

CytoNiche has developed an automated and scalable solution using proprietary 3D microtissue engineering technology to address the pain points faced by live-cell manufacturing companies. Not only does the technology help increase the treatment efficiency but it also substantially reduces the cost of consumables, labor, infrastructure, and time.

"What we saw was that there wasn't anyone developing specialized microcarriers for stem cells that would allow mass production," said Dr. Yan. "This is where we could utilize our patented tissue engineering technology." What's unique about CytoNiche's technology is that it enables stem cell production at scale by combining existing pharmaceutical methods from antibody production with the domain of stem cells.

3D Microtissue Engineering Technology

CytoNiche's original patented technology, 3D microtissue engineering, allows for large-scale manufacturing of adherent cells with automated systems. It is an automated live-cell mass manufacturing platform to increase manufacturing and treatment efficiency.

Compared to traditional methods of live-cell manufacturing, this proprietary technology effectively produces one billion cells with just one worker in 15 days. This translates into savings of 80% in labor cost, 90% in infrastructure rents, 50% in consumables, and 50% in time.

More importantly, it can be used to formulate stem cells during cell therapy to improve therapeutic effects, also known as microtissue therapy.

By incorporating CytoNiche's technology into production lines, companies can ramp up live-cell production.

Currently, CytoNiche's 3D microtissue engineering is commercialized into two products:

(1) **3D TableTrix®**

The 3D TableTrix® is CytoNiche's best-in-class, dissolvable excipient-grade microcarrier (see Figure 2). These microcarriers allow stem cells to elevate from a 2D planar culture system to a 3D bioreactor system, so that cell culture can be fully automated, making cell production much simpler.

3D TableTrix® comes in a patented tablet design. Each tablet is composed of tens of thousands of elastic 3D porous microcarriers. These microcarriers have a porosity level of more than 90%, the size of the particles can be controlled at a range of 50–500 μm, and uniformity is recorded at ≤100 μm. The biochemical and physical properties can be customized to form an authentic 3D bionic culture. Additionally, these microcarriers are fully biodegradable. Hence, cells cultured on these microcarriers can be fully recovered. With these excipient-grade microcarriers, injecting them into the human body is considered safe.

Figure 2: CytoNiche's 3D TableTrix® microcarriers.

(2) **3D FloTrix®**

3D TableTrix® allows cells to be elevated to 3D culture, making stem cell culture in automated bioreactors feasible (see Figures 3 and 4). Hence, 3D FloTrix®, a patented process for automated cell culture incorporating various scalable bioreactors, automated cell washing, concentration, and filling equipment, allows for scaling up with a small footprint compared to 2D planar culture systems conventionally used for stem cell production.

These bioreactors and automated cell processing equipment can be automatically controlled, so there is no need for more workers even if the production scale is increased. There is also less reliance on the operator's expertise to manufacture high-quality cells, thus simplifying stem cell mass production.

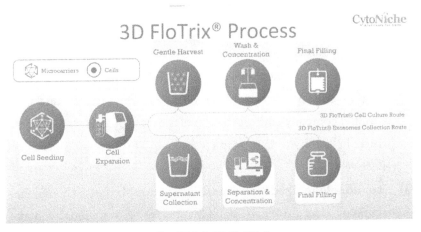

Figure 3: CytoNiche's 3D FloTrix® process.

Figure 4: CytoNiche's 3D FloTrix® process design application.

What Makes CytoNiche Stand Apart?

(1) **Best-in-class Microcarrier Suppliers**: CytoNiche's microcarriers are the best in class in large-scale live-cell production since they enable high cell yield. At the same time, competitors in the market have yet to introduce pharmaceutical-grade products. CytoNiche had previously created an upstream technology and product focusing on the downstream biopharmaceutical market. Furthermore, CytoNiche's technology outperforms its competitors in terms of dissolvability scale. Because competitors' products are non-dissolvable, cell harvesting from their microcarriers is inefficient. Non-pharmaceutical-grade goods, on the other hand, are not suitable for direct injection into the human body. CytoNiche's 3D TableTrix® is safe to inject *in vivo* for therapy. As such, microtissue therapy is made possible. The standalone medical device is used as a delivery system for stem cells to improve therapeutic effects.

(2) **Complete Solutions and Services**: CytoNiche acts as a supplier and a contract development and manufacturing company to effectively integrate cell culture harvesting, filling systems, and products. As such, the company controls the cellular drugs' process development which helps customers produce high-quality and safe products effectively.

(3) **Expandable to Traditional and Emerging Markets**: CytoNiche's technology has also been adopted and applied to various products, including vaccine production, gene therapy, cosmetics, lab-produced milk, clean meat, exosomes, bioartificial livers, hematopoietic stem cells, protein production, cosmetics, and aesthetic medicine.

The Business Model

Target Market

Biochemical companies, pharmaceutical companies, and other live-cell manufacturers looking to scale up their production capacities while keeping products affordable for patients are important stakeholders and partners for CytoNiche. Specifically, CytoNiche focuses on companies in the regenerative medicine field responsible for cell and genetic therapies.

Affirmation

Since its incorporation in 2018, CytoNiche has raised over USD60 million. Its R&D and sales center in Beijing spans 3,000 m², and its production facility in Tianjin occupies 4,000 m².

Through its upstream technology and product, CytoNiche has launched pharmaceutical-grade products, giving it a first-mover advantage over its competitors. In addition, CytoNiche has secured more than 60 patents, including 30 granted patents, three Patent Cooperation Treaty (PCT) patents, and eight international patents under filing, to enhance its market value and gain a competitive edge over other firms.

The company was granted four copyrights and 37 trademarks. More impressively, its comprehensive solution and services have helped achieve more than a 500% increase in sales in 2021. With more than 100 customers, including 50% of the mesenchymal stem cell therapy companies that have filed for Investigational New Drug (IND) in China and more than ten distributors, under its portfolio, the efficacy of CytoNiche's patented 3D microtissue engineering technology has been repeatedly proven.

Revenue Model

When CytoNiche first started in 2018, it adopted a razor-and-blade business model where manufacturers would purchase its bioreactors while paying a recurring fee for microcarriers used and disposed of in each batch of cell production. Fast-forward to 2021, CytoNiche's revenue comes from three sources — Consumables and Equipment, Contract Development and Manufacturing, and Microtissue Drugs.

CytoNiche is potentially an exclusive and long-term supplier of its patented cell manufacturing systems to more than 50% of China's mesenchymal stem cell therapy companies that have filed for IND. The company has also launched its contract manufacturing services to supply stem cell drug development services, ready-made cells, or cell-derived products like exosomes and microtissue therapy drugs for chronic diseases.

Insights

Back in 2015, when the idea of CytoNiche was born, the founders spent the better part of the following three years talking to investors and experts. Unfortunately, with a lack of regulatory clarity in China around how stem cells should be produced, it was challenging to convince investors to fund stem cell projects.

It wasn't until 2018 that the Chinese Food and Drug Administration (FDA) came up with clear guidelines on regulating stem cells the same way as they do for other pharmaceutical drugs. This was great news for CytoNiche because this development enabled its launch.

> *We all had the technical know-how, but we never talked about business models or who might buy our product.*
> — **Dr. Xiaojun Yan**, Co-Founder and CTO

The team contacted alumni connections at Tsinghua University, many of whom were successful entrepreneurs. Another source was a start-up incubator at the university, which connected them with experts, such as patent lawyers. The university's Technology Transfer Office also offered advice, especially getting approval from the relevant government ministries. "These research grants are very good funding sources for biotech startups because they are usually easy to get for teams with hardcore technology, and often you don't have to pay them back," said Dr. Yan.

Early-stage angel investors, she said, often had great confidence in CytoNiche's technology. As a result, the team didn't need to reveal secrets in these conversations about how the core technology worked; instead, they focused on what it could be used for.

"Early on, we have decided what information we will publicly talk about, and what not to, to investors," said Dr. Yan. For example, when the team didn't want to answer an investor's question, they went to a standard reply: "We need to ask our Ph.D. supervisor about this."

The company also holds several successful patent applications and trade secrets. The patent strategy was a conscious decision for CytoNiche. They made sure to synchronize the filing of the patents with the company's efforts. It took a deliberate three years of effort to have all the patents in place, but it was well worth the time.

Looking Ahead

Accolades in China have helped CytoNiche gain recognition as a national high-tech firm. Having received a revolutionary technology grant from Zhongguancun (ZGC), CytoNiche will have launched two clinical trials in 2022.

Driven by the cell therapy or regenerative medicine market, the cell culture market is projected to be worth USD40 billion by 2027. The cell therapy market is expected to increase by a compounded annual growth rate of 11–15%. With revenues streaming in from consumables and equipment, contract development, manufacturing, and its microtissue drugs, the company's focus on the cell therapy market could very well pay off in the future. CytoNiche is also set to establish its wider footprint worldwide as the outlook remains positive for global regenerative medicine.

We at CytoNiche are serious about large-scale 3D manufacturing of high-quality cells.

— **Dr. Xiaojun Yan**, Co-Founder and CTO

CHAPTER 5

Iterative Scopes: Intelligence and Precision for Gastrointestinal Health

What would you do if I told you that your life depended on your doctor's ability to find a polyp in your colonoscopy test?
— **Dr. Jonathan Ng**, Founder and CEO, Iterative Scopes

terative Scopes is on a mission to improve people's health and well-being by enhancing the detection of gastrointestinal diseases with the introduction of artificial intelligence into the field of gastroenterology. Primarily focused on the gastroenterology industry, Iterative Scopes leverages artificial intelligence to create precision software for detecting gastrointestinal diseases and improving gastrointestinal health. Iterative Scopes has made significant contributions to health and well-being within four years of its starting up and is set to be a game-changer in its field globally.

When 16-year-old Jonathan (Jon) Ng visited post-Khmer Rouge Cambodia and saw the state of rural hospitals, he decided he wanted to improve the state of healthcare for those that needed it most. He pursued medicine first at the National University of Singapore (NUS), then at MIT and Harvard in the USA. His studies took him around the globe to some of the best hospitals and research facilities in the world. The differences in medical care, and the variation in skill and quality, were very clear. So, Dr. Ng challenged himself to push past the boundaries of the healthcare industry. He started to raise funds to build a hospital specializing in open-heart surgery for kids, a project he championed for some 14 years.

He spent five years in a rigorous medical school program to qualify as a medical officer. A surgeon by training, he saw the larger issues at play in healthcare and how the model that existed made diagnostic equipment, medical tests, and, thus, relevant information inaccessible to many of the people who needed it most. He was compelled to pursue his passion and try to bridge gaps in the healthcare field, with a focus on his area of expertise — the gastrointestinal field.

After enrolling in MIT to study business and Harvard for further studies in healthcare policy, Dr. Ng went on leave to test out his idea of offering improved accessibility to patients across the board. Today, he is the founder and CEO of Iterative Scopes, the leader in computational gastroenterology.

In pioneering the application of powerful, proprietary artificial intelligence tools to the practice of gastroenterology and drug development, he helps provide doctors with real-time computer-aided detection and diagnostic tools to improve patient outcomes. At the same time, another company he founded, Optimimed, gave patients in public hospitals a means to access specialized equipment without waiting months for an MRI.

By having them take advantage of downtimes in private practices, he not only reduced institutional excess capacity and patient wait times but also made it possible for patients to receive MRI scans more quickly, without having to pay extra for the service. This resulted in cost savings for patients, who got healthcare they wouldn't otherwise have been able to afford.

Problem and Opportunity: Analyzing the Videos

Defensible Data

Minimal research has been done to analyze colonoscopy videos or provide efficient access to essential images and video segments from colonoscopy videos. Despite a large body of knowledge in medical image analysis, very little research has also been done to investigate automatic measurement methods to evaluate the quality of the colonoscopic procedure.

Additionally, most hospitals do not record or store colonoscopy videos, despite the richness of data present while physicians view them. As such, Jon decided to start his journey by de-risking the technology in a simple way — by helping physicians detect colorectal cancer polyps.

De-risking Technology with Polyp Detection

In gastroenterology, the detection and classification of polyps are highly intuitive and user-dependent on practitioners themselves. According to the National Cancer Institute, a polyp is defined as "a growth that protrudes from a mucous membrane."[1] In layman's terms, it is what we recognize as a "tumor." Adenomatous polyps, also known as adenomas, are a common type of polyp, usually benign or precancerous.

The Adenoma Detection Rate (ADR) is a quality indicator of colonoscopy screening. It is defined as "the rate at which a physician finds one or more precancerous polyps during a normal screening colonoscopy procedure for patients over 50 years old."[2] In essence, the higher the ADR, the better the medical practitioner. A practitioner's ability to detect polyps reflects the quality of the colonoscopy screening and represents a lower

---

[1] https://www.cancer.gov/publications/dictionaries/cancer-terms/def/polyp.
[2] https://www.ncbi.nlm.nih.gov/pmc/articles/PMC8106918/.

chance of polyps becoming cancerous. ADR varies widely among medical practitioners. The disparity in ADR or detection of polyps can be attributed to the following:

(1) **Expertise and Experience**: There is a significant variation in ADR and quality of colonoscopy screening among different medical specialties. While the minimal ADR rate quality has been set at 25% for a screening colonoscopy, many physicians not only fail to achieve this rate but also find it difficult to understand if they are hitting these targets. The wide variation in training throughout the world also underscores the reason why physicians and, in turn, patients have such differences in ADR outcomes.

(2) **Quality of Performance**: In a perfect world, performance should remain consistent regardless of circumstance. However, we live in an imperfect world. When "bad" days hit, we are affected no matter how much we try not to be — and there is nothing wrong with not feeling ourselves; it is all part of the human experience. But what do you do when you work with life and death, and you cannot afford to make mistakes? In reality, the process of colonoscopy screenings and detecting polyps will never be an exact replication of any previous version. Various circumstances affecting medical practitioners can hinder their performance and ability to detect polyps. However, the accuracy around the detection process can be improved with the right intelligence tools.

Advancing Technology Through Inflammatory Bowel Disease

In the practice of gastroenterology, treatments are highly heterogeneous — that is, different patients need to receive different medical treatments based on their specific situations. A one-size-fits-all approach is not sufficient. This is especially true in the case of patients with complex chronic diseases like inflammatory bowel disease.

Every patient's [Inflammatory Bowel Disease] is different, so a
personalized approach is key.
— UChicago Medicine

Without the ability to use meaningful predictive models to help medical practitioners detect polyps and evaluate the severity of individual bowel disease, treatment is at risk of failing, and these diseases are at risk of unchecked progression.

In fact, some USD6 billion is spent unnecessarily every year on bowel disease diagnostics due to suboptimal tracking and therapeutic assignments. Gastrointestinal data software is currently used to improve the detection of two common medical conditions:

(1) **Colorectal Cancer**: Colorectal cancer, or colon cancer, is the second most common cancer and the second leading cause of cancer-related deaths in the United States.[3] Early colonoscopy screening can help detect precancerous polyps (see Figure 1) and reduce the risk of them becoming cancerous. For every 1% increase in ADR, one can expect a 3% reduction in the cancer risk.

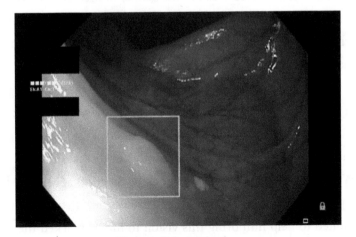

Figure 1: Colorectal polyp.

---

[3] https://www.cdc.gov/cancer/colorectal/statistics/index.htm.

(2) **Inflammatory Bowel Disease:** An estimated 2% of the world's population lives with inflammatory bowel disease. Inflammatory bowel disease occurs when the human body identifies the bowel as a foreign object, causing inflammation to the gastrointestinal tract.

Traditional methods of detection involve sending recorded videos to expert readers who primarily identify features present in the colon to determine the severity of the disease. This approach is neither quantifiable nor repeatable. However, machine learning models are central features of modern-day scientific methods.

Solution

Iterative Scopes uses state-of-the-art machine learning to help gastroenterologists detect and classify lesions in the human gut in real time, including those that often elude the human eye.

Dedicating all his time to healthcare, Dr. Ng had never really explored the business realm. It was only through a conversation with a mentor of his, Professor Hooi, a Vice-Dean of the School of Medicine at NUS, that he realized the MBA path was a possibility. After a good amount of research, Jon decided to pursue an MBA at MIT. It was during his time at MIT that Dr. Ng stumbled upon computer vision and was instantly drawn to how malleable, adaptive, and incredibly intuitive the technology was to him as a practitioner. Dr. Ng wondered, "If these algorithms could recognize and utilize prior information to classify a cat from a dog from a human, why not various subtypes of tumors or diseases?"

With that realization, he began knocking on doors at MIT. He found a lot of generosity within his personal and professional network — people who wanted to help him bring this vision to life. He picked the easiest proof point imaginable — the detection of polyps during colonoscopies through SKOUT™ (see Figure 2).

SKOUT™ reduces the subjectivity around polyp detection and the lack of a good predictive model. This artificial intelligence toolkit provides real-time actionable insights for medical practitioners. It empowers medical practitioners to better detect and classify polyps precisely with less reliance on a practitioner's subjective diagnosis and enables medical practitioners to better select the correct treatment for patients.

Trained by the world's best and most experienced gastrointestinal specialists, deep neural networks continuously engage in unsupervised learning to mimic the best human brains. In this sense, polyp detection becomes more accurate and thorough as the machine learning model recognizes hidden patterns and helps identify polyps that would otherwise likely evade detection.

Iterative Scopes' artificial intelligence software includes a colorectal cancer prevention algorithm that helps to detect polyps in real time. It is a simple, fuss-free, plug-and-play application. By plugging the endoscope into the gastrointestinal software during a screening procedure, the software can process the image and video stream in real time to detect polyps. SKOUT™ takes only 17 milliseconds to detect and classify polyps, which does not affect the standard procedure at all. In a study of 1,000

Figure 2: SKOUT™, an artificial intelligence toolkit for polyp detection.

patients, SKOUT™ was found to have helped increase the detection of precancerous polyps by 74% compared to medical practitioners. Significantly, this translates to a 50% risk reduction for potential colorectal cancer patients and better healthcare progression.

With the help of the SKOUT™ artificial intelligence software, more than 20 clinical features related to inflammatory bowel disease can be detected from a patient's endoscopic view. More importantly, its computer vision algorithms can intelligently quantify the severity of the inflammatory bowel disease and compare it across time to determine its progression. Apart from a more exhaustive screening and precise detection procedure, it enables practitioners to provide proper and timely care, reducing the severity of the disease.

Integrated Database

Iterative Scopes aims to build an ultimate integrated inflammatory bowel disease database containing proprietary visual data collected by SKOUT™, data retrieved from clinical trials, medical partners, and data around patients. By combining the vast amount of data, extensive profiles of patients can be stored in the database, forming a predictive analytics interface.

> *We have larger volume and greater depth of data than our competitors. Mind you, not just any data, but data that is well organized, integrated, and carefully curated. We are building the ultimate gastrointestinal database.*
> — **Dr. Jonathan Ng**, Founder and CEO, Iterative Scopes

With artificial intelligence, the database helps to improve polyp detection and ensures the right therapeutics are provided to individual patients based on their medical histories and health conditions. Notably, this database could provide valuable information and become a source for suitable patients for potentially successful clinical trials.

The Business Model

Target Market

The colorectal cancer and inflammatory bowel disease markets are worth USD1 billion and USD6.5 billion, respectively. With the market expected to expand 8.5% year on year despite the COVID-19 pandemic, Iterative Scopes has a substantial opportunity to capitalize on this and grow its market presence.

Pharmaceutical companies, medical practitioners from various specialties, and patients are important stakeholders and partners for Iterative Scopes. While Iterative Scopes' gastrointestinal software is intended to help medical practitioners and patients, the company hopes to attract the attention of large pharmaceutical companies. This is because individual medical practitioners tend to view the software as expensive and unaffordable. Comparatively, pharmaceutical companies have immense purchasing power and can afford the costly software and deploy it within healthcare facilities. Currently, this software is used in more than 50 centers across the US and, by the end of 2022, software developed by Iterative Scopes is estimated to be deployed in some 300 centers across the USA.

Affirmation

Iterative Scopes has a tremendous pipeline of partners involved in developing and delivering its products to the market. Its software is being delivered to some of the largest electronic health record companies, including key partners such as Minneapolis, MN-based Provation Medical.

Iterative Scopes has gone on to raise approximately USD200 million to date and grown its headcount from 20 to 170 within a 12-month period. For a four-year-old company, such remarkable achievements point to the viability of the solutions offered by the company.

Revenue Model

Iterative Scopes adopts a usage-based subscription model for endoscopic scoring per video read cost. Iterative Scopes' estimated annual revenue is around USD5 million. It recently raised USD150 million in Series B financing to accelerate the development of its core algorithmic innovations designed to transform gastroenterology care for patients. Iterative Scopes works toward narrowing the disparities in patient outcomes through artificial intelligence — starting with inflammatory bowel disease and colorectal cancer — with the potential to create novel endpoints that are better predictors of therapeutic response and disease outcomes.

Insights

Critical Milestones

Leaving an academic environment to pursue the development of Iterative Scopes was not easy, but Dr. Ng knew that this was his opportunity. Despite not knowing much about businesses, start-ups, or investors, he decided to take a leap of faith. "I didn't know what a VC was until after I started a company," he offered during a recent interview.

Dr. Ng credits part of his success to the community and network that he grew up with. For him, it was about having the correct mindset, he explains, adding that he was pursuing philanthropy in Cambodia for many years alongside a very entrepreneurial community.

Still, while the desire to help others was there, realistically scaling the business to make a greater impact required resources and a sustainable business model. As such, Dr. Ng had to learn to pitch and sell his idea to people who could take his passion to the next level.

Asking for money on a philanthropic basis is different from forecasting returns, and there was a lot of selling and convincing people that the idea can work.
— **Dr. Jonathan Ng**, Founder and CEO, Iterative Scopes

There was a lot of uncertainty, but Dr. Ng stuck to his guns, continued to learn, and stayed agile enough to adapt. "You figure it out along the way," he says.

Challenges

Attending two schools and running two companies at the same time posed a huge challenge in time management. Dr. Ng was a fish out of the water with no idea of how VCs worked, no experience in tech, and no clue about what a product manager does, trying to build a tech company with his solution to a very real problem. He wanted to pitch to potential investors and look for the right people to support the idea.

"As someone who was constantly striving to achieve the highest accolades, I was used to more 'Yeses' than 'Nos.' 2018 was incredibly tough for us," he explains. However, "this teaches you resilience," he elaborates.

Entrepreneurs need to be able to rely on a whole secondary group of people who are willing to support their agenda and objectives but, most importantly, be there when they need to support the vision. As much as it would have been nice to walk out with a giant check, Dr. Ng believes that their success came from hard work and their culture was formed from grit.

As a founder, your priority is to make sure that your decisions are not catastrophic.
— **Dr. Jonathan Ng**, Founder and CEO, Iterative Scopes

Looking Ahead

Dr. Ng has since grown his company to 170 people and, as the company grew, so did the problems along the way. Communication breakdowns, market and investor uncertainty during the COVID-19 crisis, and dealing with rejection were all issues Dr. Ng had to face.

Feeling like the business took off rather slowly, Dr. Ng still believes in hard work and constant learning. "Failing is actually very helpful and making mistakes early is key," he says.

With growth, Dr. Ng felt that there were times when communication was a huge challenge. There were instances where he would mention something in passing, and someone would take a memo on it, causing the team to work on something that was perhaps not in the pipeline. The opposite would also occur, and product specifications would be completely off. He says miscommunication was the root cause behind many challenges that he had to overcome.

Dr. Ng stressed that you need people you can trust to carry out critical roles, and people need to be aligned with the leadership. Being a solo founder also meant that he had to rely on people to make decisions at every level. With this comes ensuring that everyone is rowing in the same direction. According to Dr. Ng, healthcare as a system is hard to change, but you can bring about substantial changes with the right tools and opportunities.

"We have jetpacks, rocket fuel, and the opportunity to go to the moon. It is up to us to make a difference," he says.

CHAPTER 6

Polybee: Using Autonomous Micro-Drones to Boost Pollination

L ike many entrepreneurs, Mr. Siddharth Jadhav's journey to starting his own company began accidentally — in his case, literally, in 2018. He had fractured his arm during a cricket match and was recovering at his parents' home in India when he picked up Yuval Harari's bestseller, *Sapiens: A Brief History of Humankind* (Harari, 2014).

The book argued that agriculture was a misstep in the evolutionary history of *homo sapiens* due to its negative impact on their nutritional profile, he recalled. Struck by its message, he soon found himself seeking a way to improve food security, especially for the world's most vulnerable people.

There was only one issue — as an aerodynamics engineer, he knew nothing about agriculture. After finishing his bachelor's degree with Honors from the Birla Institute of Technology and Science in India in 2016, Siddharth went to Singapore to work as a research engineer at the National University of Singapore (NUS). However, he always looked to graduate school in the United States, where he planned to earn a Ph.D. in aerodynamics.

Putting that aside, he "took a shot in the dark," as he calls it, and deferred his admission to graduate school. What he sought was an opportunity that could change people's lives through agricultural innovation. One area in which he could use his expertise was developing the deep tech and artificial intelligence to use small drones to pollinate crops like strawberries, tomatoes, and pepper; in other words, turn them into "smart" mechanical bees.

To do this, in 2019, he assembled the necessary pieces of the puzzle while he was still in Singapore. This was the beginning of Polybee, a start-up with a mission to enhance global food security with the promise of advances in robotics and artificial intelligence (AI). Polybee wasn't the first to explore this new field. Other companies before Polybee had also looked to innovative artificial pollination solutions for the long-standing issues that farmers have been facing.

Weighing his options, Siddharth decided that drones were the best way forward to solve this problem at scale. The main engineering issue involved "de-risking the drones" to reduce mid-air collisions, damage to property, and loss of control. The concept needed to be tested.

Around this time, the Singapore Food Agency (SFA) announced a new strategic goal to transform the country's agri-food industry into one that produces 30% of the nation's nutritional needs locally by 2030.

Siddharth sent the agency a cold email asking for support. A positive reply soon came, and he was given a small plot of an indoor strawberry plantation to test out his idea. At this point, the pollinating micro-drones only existed in concept and needed much experimentation to create the first working prototype.

But, as the saying goes, that was the spark that lit the flame. Temasek Foundation, the philanthropy arm of Temasek Holdings Singapore, saw the initial results from the SFA strawberry field trials and decided to fund the project in hopes of scaling the technology.

With support from NUS and Temasek Foundation, Polybee was built up gradually. The accelerator program at the university de-risked the venture for Siddharth and mitigated many of his worries, such as entering a new world of agriculture. This allowed him to focus on building the product and the business without worrying about whether he had to quit his job or figure out how he was going to pay his bills while he worked on this problem.

Problem and Opportunity: A Better Way to Farm

The need to feed a growing population around the world has led to urgent calls for better food security, in particular, for the most vulnerable. The uneven recovery from the COVID-19 pandemic, war, and climate change have also disrupted the supply of food sources and final products, according to the United Nations.[1]

For the agriculture sector, improving the way crops are farmed is one important way to overcome today's many challenges to food supply.

Production Deficit

First, there is a production deficit. Like the production of any kind of product, farming faces challenges with productivity. The production of crops is highly dependent on pollination, which in recent years has been disrupted by climate change, the encroachment of urbanization, and in places like Asia and Australia the lack of access to natural pollinators.

The Food and Agriculture Organization (FAO) of the United Nations (2022) estimates that the market of fresh produce is currently worth around USD850 billion. With efficient pollination and sufficient access to fresh fruits and vegetables, the fresh produce market is expected to achieve its full potential at a massive valuation of USD2.5 trillion.

---

[1] https://press.un.org/en/2022/sgsm21350.doc.htm, 24 June 2022.

Three main forces drive the deficit of fresh fruit and vegetable production and change the playing field:

(1) **Rising Demand for Fresh and Nutritious Produce**: Consumer preferences have been changing over the years, and consumers are actively adopting healthier food and dietary choices compared to the past. Different considerations such as health conditions, health benefits, and lifestyles influence consumers' consumption of fresh produce. This means a continued demand for high-quality fresh produce amid declining supply.

(2) **Rising Urban Population**: In less than 20 years, more than two-thirds of the world population is expected to reside in cities. However, the production of fresh fruits and vegetables tends to be concentrated in non-urbanized areas. With a more urbanized population, fresh fruit and vegetable production should also get closer to where it is consumed. Given its short shelf life, there is a need for fresh harvest to reach consumers as soon as possible. Addressing these issues, efficient pollination lets farmers grow more from less.

(3) **Climate Change and Depleting Resources**: Horticultural crops are especially vulnerable to climate change, and even the slightest change in average temperature can drastically affect the yields of fruits and vegetables. This affects the quality and quantity of harvested crops, threatening our global food supply.

Natural Pollination Constraints

Natural pollination needs no human intervention as natural pollinators, such as bees, fertilize crops. For fertilization to occur, these pollinators help to transfer the pollen from the stamen of a male flower/plant to the pistil of a female flower/plant. Fruit crops with the most significant potential all need bumblebees for pollination — from the tomatoes in a salad to the berries in smoothies, and even taken-for-granted peppers.

However, there are constraints to natural pollination:

(1) **Spread of Plant Pathogens**: Farmers often report the spread of plant pathogens by bees. An outbreak of plant disease spread by natural pollinators could greatly reduce fruit and vegetable yield.

(2) **Unavailability of Bumblebees**: Major agricultural producers in urban areas such as Asia, Africa, and Australia are turning to greenhouses and vertical farms. In these metropolitan cities, there is a lack of access to bumblebees.

(3) **Suboptimal Pollination in Non-Ideal Weather Conditions**: Bumblebees are partially endothermic insects and can generate enough heat to fly if the temperature of their environment is not too cold. However, they will not leave their hives if the weather is too cold. For natural pollination to occur, its flight muscles must be above 30°C, and its thorax during flight must be maintained between 30°C and 40°C. Even if natural pollination were to occur during cold weather, such pollination is at a suboptimal level due to the subdued foraging activity, and the quality of the product will be negatively affected.

Manual Pollination Costs

An alternative to natural pollination is manual pollination. As the term "manual" suggests, manual pollination requires human intervention and manual labor. For fertilization to occur, a manual technique is used to transfer pollen from the stamen of a male flower/plant to the pistil of a female flower/plant.

Manual pollination is not a feasible solution for the following reasons:

(1) **Expensive and Inefficient**: Manual pollination is a tedious process that incurs high costs and poor efficiency in operations. In Australia, the annual cost for manual pollination is AUD37,500 per hectare.

(2) **Time-Consuming**: Manual pollination does not stop once the pollen is transferred. After pollination, subsequent factors such as optimal inputs and climate conditions need to be considered. These are determining factors for the development of high-quality fruits and vegetables. Measurement of some parameters relating to plant health, flowering, and fruit development is required on a day-to-day basis. It takes time for sufficient data to be collected before analysis for maximum yield. In most businesses, time equals money, and requiring more time for data collection means burning more cash.

Plant Measurements Deficiency

Plant measurement is an essential tool required for breeding decisions and optimization of yield. Seeds comprise another industry that relies heavily on plant data measurements, and it is the cornerstone of food security. Most of the food consumed today is grown with hybrid seeds — a cross-pollination between two varieties of crops. It churns a higher premium and is valued at USD53 billion, with a compounded annual growth rate of 9.7% by 2026. Seed companies seek to develop new plant variants that produce higher yields while providing greater resilience to climate change and pest diseases.

Research and development of hybrid seeds and new individual variants is not as easy as it seems, because of the following challenges:

(1) **Lack of Tools**: There is a lack of digital tools to accurately measure plant traits in the current agricultural industry. In such situations, breeders can only rely on a limited workforce and subjective judgments in making breeding decisions.

(2) **Long Development Horizons**: Inadequate plant measurement tools directly affect the research and development timeline of hybrid seeds

and new individual variants. Without proper tools, a long development time is unavoidable because there are difficulties in determining plant phenotype. Generally, developing one crop variety costs millions of dollars and can take up to 10 years. However, with the right tools on hand, seed companies can save up to 30% of their development time and costs with advanced technology.

Solution

Polybee envisions that autonomous pollination can be achieved at scale with drones. Autonomous drones in controlled-environment agriculture, more commonly known as "indoor farming," in greenhouses and vertical farms, can address the identified industry problems.

Control is of paramount importance, and it is the most critical step in cultivation, allowing companies to trace and predict yields.

With the use of micro-drones to automate pollination and crop monitoring in controlled-environment agriculture, Polybee has identified three main pillars of technology:

(1) **Automation**: A fully autonomous platform is required to eliminate labor expenses and inconsistencies in research and operation.

(2) **Precision in Time and Space**: Precision in time and space is critical for pollination. Every flower has a narrow window of two to three days for optimal pollination. With the right technology, tracing and prediction planning can be done beforehand to achieve optimal yield.

(3) **High-Throughput Capacity**: The high-throughput capacity at a viable input cost allows Polybee to pollinate hundreds or thousands of flowers or plants daily.

Technologies

Three major technology pillars are critical to Polybee's solution, helping it stand out from rival offerings in the market:

(1) **Patent-Pending Pollination Method**

Polybee has developed a patent-pending method of pollination suited specifically for fruit crops such as tomatoes, berries, and peppers. The approach also addresses the "bottleneck" issue of pollination in countries where manual pollination is expensive and infeasible. Additionally, it can maximize results from natural pollination (i.e., bumblebees).

(2) **Autonomous Navigation Software for Nano-drones**

Polybee builds autonomous micro-drones to ensure precision pollination and high-throughput capacity while making economic sense.

Polybee's smallest drone is only 9 cm in size. Despite this, it is capable of precise flight through confined spaces, even in a GPS-denied indoor environment (sub-cm accuracy). More importantly, it can cover a large area in a timely yet consistent manner.

Greenhouse and vertical indoor farms are mapped out using cameras and are connected to a central AI-powered system controlling several other drones autonomously. Polybee ensures precise pollination within an error of 1 cm. The team can effectively operate one drone per 25 m² in a vertical indoor farm and about 30 drones per hectare in a greenhouse.

(3) **Computer Vision**

Polybee has developed cutting-edge 3D computer vision algorithms that enable two operations: autonomous navigation around complex structures of plants and measurement of key plant traits such as yield, plant health, and stress.

Tying these components together is Polybee's in-house-built software platform, called Phenobee. It streamlined data visualization and deployment autonomous operations for users.

Through this platform, growers and breeders can make faster and better decisions with insights delivered by the data. The autonomous drones collect high-throughput data, allowing Polybee to collect high-resolution visual data and eliminate the cost and subjectivity of manual measurements.

Phenobee also doubles up as a digital phenotyping platform. It can measure, visualize, and compare plant traits based on images through the use of bleeding-edge artificial intelligence (AI) and computer vision. Currently, Polybee offers phenotyping services for certain types of fruit, such as tomatoes, peppers, and strawberries.

Measuring effectiveness

It is important to measure how well the crops have been pollinated. Polybee utilizes two key metrics to evaluate effectiveness:

(1) **Fruit Set Rate**: Fruit set rate refers to the fraction of flowers that turn into fruits. Polybee's patented pollination method has successfully turned 90% of flowers into fruits, comparable to natural pollination by bumblebees.

(2) **Marketable Fruit Set Rate**: Marketable fruit set rate refers to the fraction of fruits that are sold to grocery stores. Polybee aims to achieve a commercial fruit set rate of 80–90% for growers, comparable to natural pollination by bumblebees.

The Business Model

What Sets Polybee Apart

Polybee adopts precision horticulture as a service to differentiate itself from its peers. Its differentiating strategies include the following:

(1) **Crop-Agnostic Services**: Polybee's technology has been validated across different crops, environments, and customers. It is taking on a massive beachhead market that spans sectors, which significantly de-risks its business.

(2) **Wide-Ranging Customers**: Polybee has a wide range of clientele such as vertical farms, seed companies, and greenhouse cooperatives with urgent agriculture issues that Polybee technologies could address and eliminate. Working with a diverse group of providers both locally and overseas has benefited Polybee rapidly, compared to working with individual growers in a particular geography.

(3) **Modular Drone: Multiple Services**: Polybee built a single-model drone platform that is tailored for pollination and plant measurements for its customers. Customers have high flexibility on the services offered for which the drones can be deployed with minor adjustments. A single, highly modular platform reduces development overheads, lowers CapEx, and improves scalability.

Target Market

Vertical farms, seed companies, and greenhouse solution providers are important stakeholders and partners for Polybee. Polybee is currently deploying its services with two Fortune 500 seed companies and is working on a follow-up contract.

Affirmation

Since its incorporation in 2019, Polybee has deployed and validated its technology with some of the biggest companies in agriculture:

(1) **Drone Pollination of Strawberries**: In early 2022, Polybee deployed its pollination feature with a major strawberry glasshouse grower in the UK. Polybee's drones helped increase yield by 50% compared to bumblebee pollination, the gold standard in the industry. Moreover, this enhancement of yield was at a time of the year when the price of the produce is the highest, whereas the natural pollinator activity is usually the lowest due to unfavorable climate.

(2) **Yield measurement**: Over the last couple of years, Polybee has proven the high-throughput capacity and the accuracy of its plant measurement service through various deployments with major seed companies in its Asia-Pacific operations. Seeing the potential of the technology in transforming plant breeding, the Europe divisions of these companies have signed up for deployments in 2022.

Revenue Model

Polybee adopts a usage-based subscription model where clients can opt for a fixed price per unit area. Besides giving control and flexibility to customers, such pay-per-use subscription plans help them directly align costs with consumption. This allows for easy onboarding of new customers looking for low-cost alternatives and does not require oversized packaged plans. More importantly, Polybee's model avoids a "one-size-fits-all" mentality and recognizes that different businesses require tailored solutions.

Insights

For Mr. Siddharth, an engineer by training, the most challenging aspect of his entrepreneurial journey is the constant switching of hats. As a start-up founder, he finds himself talking to customers, discussing product roadmaps with the team, and convincing investors to see the vision behind Polybee in the next minute.

As the first rounds of successful funding and encouraging trials started, he realized that creating a company will help him achieve his goals faster.

"I didn't really have an aspiration to become a founder," he admitted, but looking beyond the isolated technical issues, he realized that he had a sea of opportunity to solve an urgent human problem in food security.

He is grateful to two of his mentors, one who believed in him from the early days at the Lean Launchpad in NUS and encouraged him to stick with his idea and another who supported him on business development and helped coach him on managing people in a business.

"It really positively affected the quality of my problem-solving," he said. "The accelerator and my mentors allowed me to focus on the problem peacefully. I couldn't have done it without them."

Looking Ahead

As a solo founder, Mr. Siddharth Jadhav knew he could not do everything alone. One important decision he made was in hiring Ms. Vinitha Selvaraj. Siddharth met Vinitha through a LinkedIn search for "indoor positioning NUS." As it turned out, she was completing her Master's thesis just across the corridor at NUS, so he reached out to her. Now, more than two years into Polybee, she leads the computer vision team.

Polybee is set to grow in the years ahead. Despite a slowdown in global economic growth, Polybee has commercialized its yield measurement feature and is deploying its pollination feature with market-leading cooperatives in the UK and Australia.

For Siddharth, there is a little irony in Singapore, a place not known for its agriculture since its decades-long march toward urbanization, now sparking innovation in the growing of crops for the future.

"Ten years from now, it will only seem natural and obvious that the world's first scalable solution for artificial pollination was invented right here in Singapore, a nation which has to grow its food in uncertain times and a nation where adversity is often seen as an opportunity," he noted.

CHAPTER 7

ZhenRobotics: Robots for a Smart, Sustainable, and Resilient Human Society

P rimarily focused within the service industry, ZhenRobotics is constructing technologies and robotic solutions for everyday use in societies. More than just convenience, ZhenRobotics has helped enable cities to become smarter and more sustainable and resilient.

From a young age, Mr. Justin Liu had always been fascinated by robots. At just 10, he won a coding competition with a piece of software that helped his teachers. As a child, he also wrote a science fiction story describing what life would be like in a distant 2020 when humans were aided by intelligent sentient robots.

Though robots are still not sentient today, at least not in the way Mr. Liu had expected, his interest and obsession with robots have propelled him on a mission to maximize the use of everyday robots to empower societies. His company, ZhenRobotics, is now developing market-leading technologies to create robotic systems that can fulfill service duties. They are expected to be handy in service sectors, which often face a labor crunch.

As with many entrepreneurs, Mr. Liu's entry into the business world took a leap of faith. Though he could have chosen a promising academic career, he decided to withdraw from his Ph.D. in Computer Sciences studies from the Swiss Federal Institute of Technology (ETH) in Zürich in 2013 to work on a robotics and artificial intelligence project. "I knew that it [machine learning] will be a trend worth learning about," he said, "especially as I wanted to build real products and not just publish academic papers."

His peer network from Zurich was a source of inspiration. "Professors at ETH typically pursue cutting-edge research and students often establish spin-off high-tech companies," he noted. "This motivated me to move forward as well."

Studying at ETH had taught him not only academic and technical skills, but also the ambition needed in the face of setbacks. He knew his technical skills alone were not sufficient and that he also had to learn product management and to know how to lead a team toward a common goal. With this very specific goal in mind, he joined Alibaba in Hangzhou, China, in 2014 and worked as a data scientist for a year. There, Mr. Liu learned the importance of regular check-ins with team members.

"I learned that in a successful business, the priority is about constantly maintaining your relationships with your stakeholders, employees, and partners," he recalled.

ZhenRobotics is now China's first developer of self-driving robots, with an aim to revolutionize last-mile delivery. Mr. Liu worked as a CEO/ CTO and led the research and development team for the next six years, while enrolling in an MBA program at Tsinghua University.

One day, he believes, robots will indeed be more closely working alongside humans in supplementing the workforce, enabling people to do a lot more in the future. As his ZhenRobotics co-founder Mr. Met Li said, "We are not saying that we need the best technology and the most high-tech geeks. But we are doing the real application for society."

Problem and Opportunity: Tackling the Labor Crunch

High Labor Costs

In China, a typical business spends 30% of its operating costs on labor, and the service industry is no exception. There are two main drivers of high labor costs:

(1) **Shrinking Labor Force**: With a declining population, China has been experiencing a shrinking labor force since 2013. In the service sector, employees aged 25–30 make up the greatest proportion of workers. With only 15% of those in the industry being below 25, many companies find it increasingly difficult to engage in intergenerational replacement of workers, much less recruit and retain more young talents for future expansion. With the outbreak of COVID-19 and lockdown restrictions, labor supply has been further reduced.

(2) **Rising Wages**: The law of supply and demand postulates that when demand exceeds supply, there tends to be an upward swing in prices. As such, a shrinking labor force and an intensified need for young talent are pushing up labor costs.

Transmission of Cross-Infectious Diseases

Close contact between service providers and service payers is inevitable throughout the service industry. However, these contacts increase the risk of cross-infections and can become a breeding ground for diseases. Before the COVID-19 pandemic, the service industry relied heavily on humans. These services include food and logistics deliveries, housekeeping and cleaning, security and surveillance, and even everyday retail. With local authorities implementing regulations to minimize human-to-human contact during the pandemic, many businesses in the service industry struggled to stay afloat. Those that found a path forward did so through digitalization and new innovative ways to fulfill service duties in a contactless manner.

The ZhenRobotics Solution

To address the labor crunch, ZhenRobotics has designed robotic systems capable of handling service duties. In line with China's futuristic vision, ZhenRobotics' robots are expected to transform China's labor force, making use of 5G and artificial intelligence to help boost the capabilities of human resources.

Core Technologies

ZhenRobotics' core technologies form the foundation for its robotic products. Every robot is manufactured with five core technologies, with the difference lying in add-on functions that provide customizations to meet specific needs and purposes. The five core technologies are machine learning, computer vision, electronic systems, autonomous localization, and navigation:

(1) **Cloud Scheduling Brain**: All robotic systems include a cloud scheduling function. This technology allows ZhenRobotics' robots to engage in intelligent planning and dispatch for efficient deliveries through a local distribution network.

(2) **Dual Artificial Intelligence Wisdom Engine**: All robotics systems include dual artificial intelligence (AI) positioning and obstacle avoidance. This technology allows ZhenRobotics' robots to sense and navigate their environment safely.

(3) **Elevator Linkage Ability**: All robotics systems include the ability to interact with elevators. This technology allows ZhenRobotics' robots to communicate directly with an elevator system in the cloud network.

(4) **Simultaneous Localization and Mapping (SLAM)**: All robotics systems include a simultaneous localization and mapping (SLAM) construction. This technology allows ZhenRobotics' robots to recognize new environments, create maps automatically, and navigate most locations using the map generated.

(5) **Six-Wheel Drive Suspension Chassis**: All robotics systems include six-wheel independent suspension damping. This technology allows ZhenRobotics' robots to navigate any terrain with pivoting and steering of 360°, a maximum load of 200 kg, and a maximum speed of 15 km/h.

Service Robots

Built on the five core technologies, each of the three robots introduced to the market has been designed with functions that are useful for specific situations:

(1) **RoboPony Mini (Delivery)**: RoboPony is designed to handle indoor and outdoor contactless terminal delivery (see Figure 1). This delivery robot is adapted to fulfill the country's growing logistics demands amid a rise in labor costs. Besides its delivery functions, it includes an ultraviolet disinfection machine capable of disinfecting delivery parcels. Its technologies and added functions allow for more thoughtful, unmanned deliveries. More importantly, it aims to reduce the risk of human-to-human transmission and helps in China's fight against COVID-19.

Figure 1: RoboPony, the delivery robot.

Figure 2: RoboBat, the patrol robot.

(2) **RoboBat Mini (Patrol)**: RoboBat is designed to handle security-patrolling duties of public spaces with 5G and AI traceability (see Figure 2). This patrol robot can secure premises through real-time visual inspection of public spaces. After the outbreak of COVID-19, mask detections and thermal infrared temperature measurements were added on top of essential patrolling functions. The robot's technologies and added functions allow more innovative surveillance, for example, doubling up as a mobile fever-screening tool.

Figure 3: RoboWhale, the cleaning robot.

(3) **RoboWhale Mini (Cleaning)**: RoboWhale is designed to be lightweight and handle commercial floor cleaning with its sweep and wash integration (see Figure 3). This cleaning robot is adapted to clean the environment of public spaces. Besides its cleaning functions, it can purify the air and includes real-time video monitoring for intelligent patrolling. Its technologies and added functions allow for smarter, unmanned cleaning and a safer atmosphere.

The Business Model

Differentiator

With the absence of similar robots that are fit for the market in China, ZhenRobotics is the first to address the needs of various market segments with its unique selling points:

(1) **Break Indoor and Outdoor Limitations**: Robots produced by ZhenRobotics are recognized as leading mobile robots for outdoor, indoor, and elevator applications. They can cover loop areas and any terrain. Comparatively, traditional robots by competitors are restricted to either outdoor or indoor use only.

(2) **Wider Range of Activities**: Robots produced by ZhenRobotics have the ability to engage in activities that range from hundreds of kilometers to tens of floors. They can match the scope of human activities and even exceed human abilities compared to traditional robots in the market.

(3) **Higher Input and Output Ratio**: Robots produced by ZhenRobotics might be cheaper and smaller in size, but they have higher productivity rates. They can work better and faster than humans. The input–output ratio is much higher compared to human labor, thus increasing capital efficiency.

(4) **Wider Range of Applications**: Robots produced by ZhenRobotics can be customized to make them applicable for any given situation. Functions can be incorporated in the robots to fulfill supplementary purposes. So far, its core technologies have been applied to last-mile food delivery, public space patrol, commercial floor cleaning, and self-driving retail. One can look forward to many other upcoming applications and inventions.

Target Market

Government agencies, e-commerce giants, commercial companies, parks, and hospitals are important stakeholders and partners for ZhenRobotics. They include domestic and overseas governments, high-end apartments and real estate management, instant distribution and logistics groups, supermarkets and office buildings, community parks and private-owned parks, and hospital isolation zones. Additionally, major transportation hubs such as railway stations, bus stations, subways stations, and even airports have utilized ZhenRobotics' robots to improve their operational efficiencies.

Affirmation

Being the first company to produce robots with such market–product fit, ZhenRobotics benefits from the first-mover advantage of securing clients in its target market segments and building a brand reputation ahead of competitors. Domestic real estate groups and overseas takeaway giants find value from RoboWhale, its cleaning robot, as it helps to increase their capital efficiency and build competitiveness.

Having completed three financing rounds and accumulated more than CNY10 million of investment from A-share listed companies, well-known domestic institutions, Silicon Valley incubators, and well-established universities, ZhenRobotics is set for rapid growth.

Revenue Model

ZhenRobotics' revenue comes from the direct sales of its robots at high product margins of 57.03–71.43%. Replacing human labor with one robot unit helps companies increase profit by USD20,900 per year, on average.

Insights

Mr. Liu had learned an important lesson on entrepreneurship from his first start-up in Beijing — having a good technical solution was not enough. The focus should be on identifying the real human needs of clients. Failure is part of the process, and it is likely that the first idea would not work out the way one had imagined. However, it is crucial to keep going instead of giving up.

Looking Ahead

The outlook of ZhenRobotics looks promising. Service robots are booming in both China's domestic and overseas markets. In 2018, the global service robot market was worth USD0.8 billion and, by 2022, it is expected to be worth USD14.5 billion (see Figure 4). Closer to home, China's service robot market is expected to reach a valuation of USD5 billion, with more than 44,000 robots projected to be sold by 2022 (see Figure 5).[1]

The service robot market is huge and growing strongly, and the market forecast shows that public service robots will dominate China's service robot market by 2025 (see Figure 6). There is massive potential for ZhenRobotics to ramp up the production of RoboBat, its patrol robot, and create new robots that can fulfill public service responsibilities.

With over 300 core functions and 20 patents under its wing, ZhenRobotics remains an influential player in China's robot market and maintains a strong leadership in technology through its world-leading R&D capabilities. It is currently developing its fifth-generation robot. Over 70 reliable tests have been conducted, and ZhenRobotics has self-built a full-scale production line with an annual output of 5,000 units.

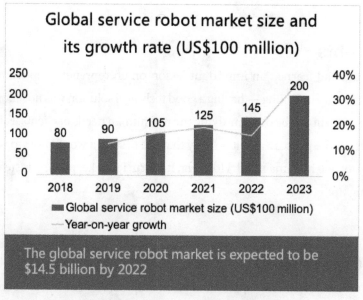

Figure 4: Global service robot market size and growth.

[1] China Electronics Society, Guotai Junan Securities.

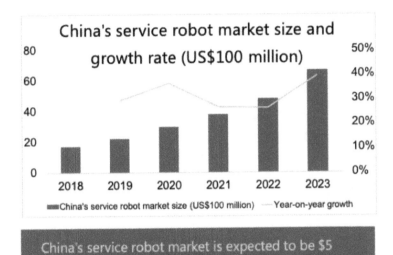

Figure 5: Service robot market size and growth in China.

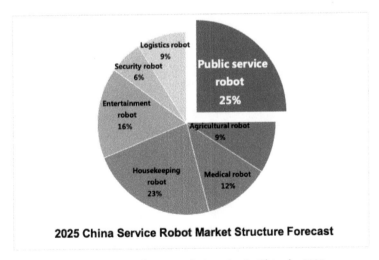

Figure 6: Forecast of service robot market in China by 2025.

With digital transformation accelerated by the COVID-19 pandemic and the need to adopt new technologies to overcome business issues, ZhenRobotics is set for rapid growth.

CHAPTER 8

Reexen: Mastering AI from Chip-Level to High-End Applications

I think when you get an idea and you think it's interesting, you can already start to meet people and then verify whether it's great or not. And mostly, don't listen to 90% of the people. Only listen to the 10% of wise people.
— **Dr. Hongjie Liu,** Founder and CEO of Reexen

Reexen is on a quest to provide low-power and energy-efficient integrated chips for the Internet of Things (IoT), reality technologies (VR/AR/MR), autonomous driving, and other smart wearable devices through its ubiquitous artificial intelligence (AI).

In 2011, founders Dr. Hongjie Liu and Dr. Xiaofeng Yang met at Nanyang Technological University (NTU) in Singapore when they were both completing their master's degrees in integrated circuit design. They went on to do internships together in Belgium at a research institute called the Interuniversity Microelectronics Centre (IMEC), which is well known for its semiconductor work. They worked on analog circuit design, which became Dr. Liu's focus on her Ph.D. research.

Dr. Liu's interest in the work of developing physical circuit boards inspired her to start a company. "It's neuromorphic processing. It's kind of mimicking how the human vision and brain compute to replace the traditional way of imaging, like processing audio signals and some image signals," she explains.

She had decided to move from an academic environment to a business environment, where these kinds of ideas could have access to the resources they'd need to grow. She next needed colleagues. "I wanted to do something big with people I like to work with," she says. "I contacted Xiaofeng (Dr. Yang) because I know we are quite complementary." He had been pursuing his Ph.D. at China's University of Macau, and, in 2019, she persuaded him to join her.

In the meantime, Dr. Yang had worked for Chinese global telecom Huawei and, during his Ph.D. studies, got to work with US-based chip maker Qualcomm. Although he had the option to work for large tech giants, he decided to join a start-up for the creativity and challenge that it offers. He was glad to hear about Liu's project in mixed signal computing. "I thought it was very interesting because it was a very new, emerging technology," he says, adding that he felt it was a growing area with a very promising future that could replace some of the computation of traditional processing units.

As a result, the pair built Reexen because they saw a market need for Internet of Things (IoT) sensors that would require a much more efficient processing flow than the conventional signal-processing chain.

Currently, Reexen operates in China and Europe, and they aim to be listed in the Chinese stock market within the next five years as a serious challenger in the global semiconductor industry. Both Dr. Liu and Dr. Yang want to scale the company and be influential rather than striving to get acquired.

Problem and Opportunity: High Performance at Low Power

The United States Semiconductor Industry Association (SIA) expects that, by 2032, there will be approximately 4.5 trillion sensors globally. These sensors are expected to generate huge amounts of data but require low power consumption while providing more flexible computing power. These upcoming IoT sensor devices would utilize conventional processor chips with low-power advanced RISC (reduced instruction set computer) machine (ARM: Advanced RISC Machines) architectures to allow a long battery life. However, traditional analog sensing and digital computing may not suit all the new algorithms that sensors need for optimal performance due to inefficiency, information redundancy, and high energy consumption.

With the problems of inefficient conversion of raw analog signals, information redundancy, and limited power supply, there was a need to create a more efficient solution to break these bottlenecks.

Inefficient Conversion of Raw Analog Signals: There are several challenges with the current way of converting raw analog signals from sensors to digital signals. A traditional converter could directly experience issues with replacing the analog front end (AFE) and the measurement of shunt voltage. Hence, converting raw analog signals from sensors to digital ones in today's age of computing is very inefficient.

Limited Power Supply: Traditional micro-controllers are not well suited to all the new algorithms that sensors require to perform on the devices. This is due to the latency and high energy consumption in analog-to-digital (A/D) conversion and data-intensive digital signal processors (DSP).

Moreover, deep neural network (DNNs) performance is often limited by memory bandwidth and processing power.

Solution

To combat the current issues faced by existing traditional analog sensing and digital computing, Reexen developed a cutting-edge chip architecture that consists of two innovations. One is analog signal processing (ASP) and the other is analog-digital mixed-signal Compute-In-Memory (CIM) (see Figure 1). Both are patented. This breakthrough architecture of in-memory computing and integrated sensing reduces the power consumption and increases its flexibility in the distribution of computing power. For Reexen, the focus is on high-energy, efficient chip design for mixed intelligence (AR/VR, robots, etc.) and IoT applications.

Energy-Efficient ASP

ASP enables edge processing directly on one's devices such as earphones and smart watches with minimum to no data transmission. It directly

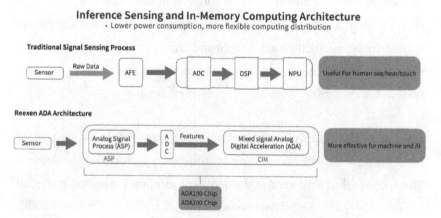

Figure 1: Traditional vs. Reexen's signal sensors.

processes the sensory signals in real time, in analog representation, and this step adds a higher level of pre-processing, extracting effective information at the sensor end. More efficient processing without a graphic processing unit (GPU) and DSP could help resolve inefficient conversions, redundant information, and limited information power supply. This greatly reduces latency and resolves high energy consumption issues in A/D conversion and data-intensive DSP.

High-Performance Mixed-Signal CIM

Apart from energy-efficient ASP, mixed-signal CIM can achieve a high performance. Reexen leverages mixed-signal computing by performing the calculations required for inference of neural networks inside a static random-access memory (SRAM) array. This represents a significant advantage over analog and typical digital architectures, breaking the "memory wall" bottleneck in conventional Von Neumann Architectures.

Reexen's CIM adopts a charge-domain computing process, which opens up opportunities for image or audio enhancement processing that cannot otherwise be implemented. Charge-domain solutions can accept IoT sensor information directly without the cost, power, and latency of digitization, and it is robust to PVT (Power, Voltage, Temperature). Therefore, it represents a better solution over both analog and digital solutions.

The processing precision can also be adjusted and customized for different application scenarios. Different processing precisions are used for voice detection and recognition, visual detection, and recognition. This is a significant technological breakthrough for the development of AR/VR, future passive/battery-powered wireless IoTs, etc.

More importantly, Reexen's innovative architecture is more effective for machines and artificial intelligence than the traditional signal-processing chain. A typical human brain has 100 billion neurons and uses only 20 watts of power to process complex signals, making it very efficient. With Reexen's architecture, the raw analog signal is converted directly into intelligence, improving efficiency, compared to the past where there was little or no feature extraction before the analog-to-digital conversion.

For Reexen, the focus is on chip design for mixed intelligence (AR/VR and robots) and IoT applications. Its unique chip architecture, which combines analog signal processing (ASP) and mixed-signal Compute-In-Memory (CIM), can deliver significantly faster results at much lower power consumption versus typical digital processors. "Our mission is to enhance the experience of people to sense and interact with the world more efficiently and smartly in the age of intelligence," Dr. Liu explains.

Products

There are currently three series of chips:

(1) **ADA10X — mass produced in 2022**: ADA100 is a time-series signal-processing chip, for applications such as voice and bio-electric signal recognition and processing, mainly for use in wearables (such as TWS headsets, smartwatches, and health-monitoring bracelets) and small IoT monitoring equipment.

(2) **ADA20X — will be mass produced in 2023**: ADA20X targets visual signal processing. This series currently consists of 2 types — the ADA200 ultra-low-power visual coprocessor and the ADA210 medium-computing-power visual system-on-chip (SoC). These can be applied to AR/VR, battery-powered IP cameras.

(3) **ADA30X — will be mass produced in 2024**: ADA30X is positioned as a high-performance SoC designed to perform multi-sensor (LiDAR plus vision) fusion signal processing. It targets the fields of AR/VR control and autonomous driving.

The Business Model

Target Market

Manufacturers of AI-based hardware are important stakeholders and partners for Reexen. Reexen targets its customers from AR/VR, AIot, autonomous driving, and robots. As of 2021, according to its co-founders, Reexen's primary market for wearable and battery-powered computing is worth USD75 billion (see Figure 2). The demand for always-on-edge computing has also been increasing and growing more robust through the years.

Affirmation

Reexen's technologies have been proven to reduce energy and silicon area cost by more than 50% and lengthen battery life of the final device by 5–10 times. Compared to traditional technologies, Reexen's products resolve heavy power consumption and offer higher performance. Furthermore, Reexen has completed two rounds of fundraising and secured USD10 million in investments from venture capital firms, which is a testament to the company's market appeal.

Figure 2: Market for wearable and battery-operated computing.

Revenue Model

Revenue from Reexen comes from three components: direct sales of audio and vision processing chips, chipset and system, as well as the IP core. Its IP core has allowed the firm to generate approximately USD100,000 to USD1 million annual earnings per company.

Insights and Challenges

The COVID-19 pandemic, which started in 2020, just 10 months after the company was officially launched, made it difficult for Reexen to market its products in Europe and in the USA as it was quite a challenge to conduct business activities then. Supply chain and manufacturing plants were all affected as well. It was difficult for the company to even pay its 20 employees their salaries. They cut employees' salaries and borrowed money from friends and family to keep their chip production underway. They sold projects and expanded their product offerings, taking on design software and hardware services to stay afloat for a year and a half before they received an investment injection of more than USD10 million from Will Semiconductor Co. Ltd. (WILLSEMI/Will Semicon), Shanghai Science & Technology Venture Capital (SHSTVC), and other investors.

Dr. Liu and Dr. Yang's ongoing teamwork has proven a success, with trust at the core of their powerful work connection. Trust is central to young entrepreneurial teams, says Dr. Liu, adding that when starting out on a new venture, it is just as important to evaluate potential co-founders on a human level as it is to understand their technical, credential-backed, skills.

As co-founders, they bring different elements to the table, but the key is trust because there's so much to do and so much reliance on each other, she says. Initially, Dr. Yang was handling the technical affairs of the firm and its operations, while Dr. Liu was focusing on the business side of things, such as investors and marketing. They seldom had the time to talk about topics like company culture and management style.

Referencing her experience with running the company with Dr. Yang, Dr. Liu notes that she trusted him and knew that they could work well together because they shared the same vision, not just the technical background. "Dr. Yang makes me feel calm, and we are both optimistic, with the same goals," she says.

Funding

Navigating funding was another major challenge. As an early mover in the Compute-in-Memory (CIM) industry, Dr. Liu fielded many questions about Reexen's competitive advantage when she spoke with potential investors. Having expected these questions, she was prepared, and spoke clearly and precisely about her goals and the company's differentiators.

Leadership

Dr. Liu was eager to focus on the product and building the company. However, as a woman in a position of leadership, she also had to prove herself to potential investors as a leader. Some thought she was not experienced enough to manage a company; others questioned if she would leave the company if she got married. Still, she persevered, explaining repeatedly that she was dedicated to growing the business for years to come. She continued to chase her dream, working hard to grow the team and business. Dr. Liu ignored the naysayers and persisted.

Dr. Liu had to respond to questions about what some potential investors perceived as a lack of business experience, since she'd come to the role from academia, not industry. Adaptive and industrious, she answered each question patiently with information about the product/market fit and how she was choosing the right team members. Tackling these tough questions gave her a chance to think through each element of the business and her role in it. She walked potential investors — and others with doubts — through the new technology, explaining that new technology often comes from academia. "Yes, we may lack the director level experience," she would tell them. "But, as former academics, our learning capability is strong."

In 2019, Dr. Liu and Dr. Yang further divided up their responsibilities, with Yang focusing on cutting-edge research around mixing traditional circuit design with new ways inspired by the human brain, while Liu handled the public-facing aspects of their business. "Among a group of engineers, I am the outgoing one and Dr. Yang is the classical quiet type," Dr. Liu admits with a smile.

Looking Ahead

Primarily focused within the semiconductor industry, Reexen is reshaping AI-based hardware. Since its inception in 2022, Reexen has closed more than USD20 million worth of orders in China and Europe in the automotive and IoT markets. By 2024, it is projected to receive in excess of USD40 million in orders and penetrate new markets in AR/VR and automotive markets.

Recognizing the positive outlook in the always-on-edge computing market, Reexen is planning to expand within Europe and China through potential collaboration with foreign partners in the coming years, despite the COVID-19 pandemic that has been affecting their business.

Within three years, Reexen has reduced energy consumption with its high-performance mixed-signal AI acceleration chips. Undeterred by obstacles, Dr. Yang leaves an encouraging message for fellow entrepreneurs. "We should be more persistent, especially when experiencing some difficult times. It is important to remain optimistic during such challenges."

In the next few years, the new application-specific integrated circuits (ASICs) are expected to lower the power consumption needed to run a DNN, allowing new cutting-edge architectures and embedded DNN functions in low-power IoT sensors. This will bolster new capabilities such as data analytics integrated with sensors and image/speech recognition in low-cost battery-powered devices, aligning with Reexen's product offerings. This further justifies the feasibility of its solutions.

Dr. Liu and Dr. Yang aim to grow the company from its current 70 headcount to a 200–300 headcount, and they plan to properly manage a team of such a size. They have plans for global expansion alongside their continued presence as the market leader in the high-efficiency inference sensing field by collaborating with bigger names and working to evolve with them.

CHAPTER 9

Emmay: Sustainable Alternative Protein via Mushroom Technology

Hit by bankruptcy about a decade ago, Ms. Pham Hong Van's family turned to a modest but delicious dish to make ends meet during difficult times. Shiitake mushroom floss, made from the family kitchen, helped bring in income and gradually lifted the family from grave financial hardship.

Buoyed by the early success, the Pham family then started selling mushroom-based products, which turned out to be a hit with the people of Hanoi, Vietnam, where they were based. A company, Emmay — We Balance, was later set up in 2017, and it quickly went beyond selling mushroom-based products to creative, green instant foods like snacks, confectionaries, and drinks.

Today, the source of plant-based nutrition that once helped pull the Pham family out of hardship has inspired Ms. Pham (Van) to create alternative protein-based food products for a sustainable future. As Emmay's CEO, she wants the company to improve global food security by producing alternative protein-based products using its mushroom biomass and mycelium technology.

This means answering the demands of a growing population that is beginning to raise alarm bells of unsustainable food demand in the decades ahead. Just as important as feeding everyone is ensuring the environment does not get destroyed by planting more crops or rearing more animals. The way forward has to be different, Van believes.

Despite knowing close to nothing about running a business at the start, she was familiar with what's required to overcome challenges — she used to get out of bed at 2 am every day to make the mushroom floss and lug up to 100 kg of dried mushrooms on her old motorbike from a farm to her home.

Emmay's ingredients are from local Vietnamese markets, which deliver high quality and freshness. The partnership also ensures local farmers and people on the lower rungs of society (single mothers, poor, uneducated, and disabled persons) can be uplifted through their labor.

Problem and Opportunity: A Momentous Challenge

The world population is expected to reach 9.8 billion by 2050, gravely impacting the environment and the nutritional health of food consumed by people.[1] This represents a complex challenge as well as an opportunity for the agri-food sector.

Unsustainable Food Demand: According to the United Nations, the food and other agricultural products market is projected to increase by 50% in the next 37 years due to positive population growth, urbanization, and a rising per capita income. The rising demand could outpace the current supply of food production, which would ultimately exhaust the planet's natural resources.

---

[1] https://www.un.org/en/desa/world-population-projected-reach-98-billion-2050-and-112-billion-2100.

Environmental Impacts on Food Production: By 2050, the use of agricultural land, water, forests, and fisheries production is forecasted to increase substantially to meet the growing demand of an increasing population. However, the inaccessibility of available land caused by the lack of infrastructure, its physical isolation and disconnection from markets, and its susceptibility to disease outbreaks could hinder the increase in agricultural land use. The environmental impacts of expanding food and agricultural production include increased land use, greenhouse gas emissions, growing freshwater usage, loss of biodiversity, and eutrophication.

Impact on Food Consumption: Approximately 100 million hectares of additional land will be required for agricultural production from now to 2050. The increase in land use could result in an increasing loss of biodiversity for food, putting food security and nutrition at risk. Incorporating a diversity of food species in one's diet is crucial to promoting health and helping to protect against diseases. The loss of agricultural biodiversity could threaten one's health, livelihood sustainability, and food and nutrition security in the future.

Solution
Rethinking Food Supply

Rethinking how food is generated and supplied is now one of the world's most important tasks. With its expertise in plant-based products, Emmay's answer is through fermenting fungi spores to create mycelium, mycoprotein, and cellulose to produce alternative plant-based meat products. Next, the strains undergo bio-fermentation, which will convert carbohydrates into protein. Finally, the formulated proteins are added to

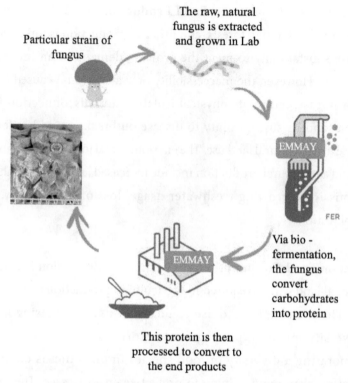

The raw, natural
fungus is extracted
and grown in Lab

Particular strain of
fungus

EMMAY

FER

Via bio -
fermentation,
the fungus
convert
carbohydrates
into protein

EMMAY

This protein is then
processed to convert to
the end products

Figure 1: Illustration of Emmay's production flowchart.

Emmay's alternative meats and green products. Its production flowchart is shown in Figure 1.

Mushrooms were selected as the core ingredient to replace animal meat and food because Emmay's research team has had 10 years of experience in research and development in biomass and mycelium technology. Through successful experimenting, Emmay created a fibrous structure resembling animal meat muscle fiber (see Figure 2). In addition, the team discovered various kinds of mushrooms with better health benefits and nutrients, for instance, a higher level of proteins and a sweet flavor — just like animal meat.

Figure 2: Emmay's shiitake-based meat.

Instead of focusing on the conventional methods of increasing food production, Emmay leveraged its fungi-based technology to develop an alternative protein-based product. Through its research in mushroom biomass and mycelium technology, the team realized that the fibers of several unique fungi could create tough fibrous structures resembling the texture of animal meat.

In addition, the growth of mycelium would only require 14 days to cultivate, which is shorter than the development of other plant crops, which spans 70–120 days. So, along with its health benefits, nutrients, and taste, Emmay decided that mushrooms are the best fit for their core ingredient.

The fungi-based technology extracts and grows natural fungi via bio-fermentation, converting carbohydrates into proteins. The fermentation of the fungi spores helps create mycelium, mycoprotein, and cellulose to produce alternative plant-based meat products. Formulated proteins are then added to Emmay's alternative meats and green products.

Another R&D direction for Emmay is its AI 3D food-printing project, which aims to create an improved solution from mushrooms biomass, mycelium, and mycoprotein technology. Essentially, through food printing, they customize the nutrient level, texture, and flavor in real time to create foods for people with dietary restrictions.

For example, people with diabetes who must follow a strict diet can enjoy the taste of protein typically found in meats and seafood through Emmay's plant-based products. The project combines alternative mushroom-based proteins with food printing. With customized foods, diabetes patients can enjoy their meals without worrying about their health problems.

Emmay was the only start-up that cooperated with Vietnam's Ministry of Industry and Trade in 3D food printing in 2021. The company ultimately aims to change the manufacturing of foods in Vietnam by reusing all materials discarded in the production process to create products of economic value, plus reduce the outflow of liquid and solid waste in the production process into the environment.

Emmay hopes that in the future 3D food printers can become smart chefs, smart doctors, and assistants, creating healthy yet delicious foods for people with different nutritional requirements.

The Business Model
Target Market
Emmay targets its markets by capitalizing on its technology, products, and sales system.

(1) Technology
Emmay's mushroom bio-mass technology has enabled the firm to gain a first-mover advantage in Vietnam and its surrounding regions. Not only

does the technology help reduce the cultivation time by at least ten days for a single batch of mushrooms but it also has the potential to reduce cultivation time even more for larger batches, making the entire process more efficient.

Apart from its ability to develop alternative protein, the technology can also incorporate 3D and 4D food printers to curate taste, flavor, and health benefits based on the palates of different consumers. In addition to the efficiency and efficacy of the technology, the projected cost is 10% lower than rearing and breeding animals and fish, allowing the company to price its products competitively.

(2) **Products**

Emmay has a one-of-a-kind basket of products, which includes various protein sources developed in different food and beverage products that none of its competitors can match. Additionally, the products promise textures that closely resemble animal meats and seafood.

Just as importantly, Emmay buys its ingredients from local Vietnamese markets, ensuring high quality and freshness. As a result, the company is confident of producing high-quality goods with increased nutrition and quality control.

(3) **Sales System**

Emmay has a dependable sales structure, with revenues flowing in from 200 retail shops in Vietnam and another 3,000 retail outlets with the potential to become business partners. In addition, Emmay has created a global presence in China, the EU, Singapore, Korea, Japan, and Taiwan. Emmay also uses online and e-commerce platforms to build brand and product awareness.

Revenues and Costs

Backing Emmay's approach is the strong market outlook for alternative meats and instant mushroom products (such as foods, drinks, sauces, spices, and related confectionaries). As a result, the alternative meat industry is expected to grow at a compounded annual growth rate (CAGR) of 10% from 2019 to 2029, reaching a value of USD140 billion (see Figure 3).

The mushroom industry is expected to reach a value of USD4.54 billion by 2023 with a CAGR of 8% from 2019 (see Figure 4).

The incremental growth of processed mushrooms has led Emmay to expand its product line of mushroom products with the brand name

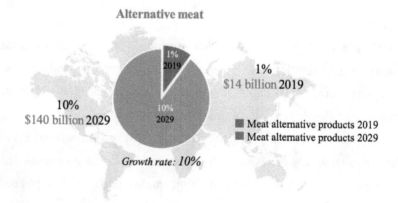

Figure 3: Projection of the market for alternative meats by 2029.

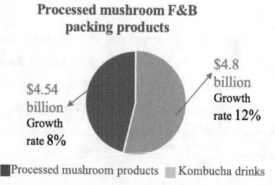

Figure 4: Projected value of mushroom products industry by 2023.

Selling + Licensing

Selling

Products line 3 (2030)
- Customizable Taste on demand
- Transfer/Licensing Tech and Recipes
- 3d Food Printer

Altenative Protein Products line 2 (since 2019)
- Alternative Pork : MVP version 01
- Alterntive Seafoods, Beef, Chicken...

Selling

Green Products line 1 (since 2010)
Creative processed foods and beverages products:
- Mushroom processed foods: Shiitale Floss, Mushrooms Sausages, Snacks....
- Musrhoom processed beverages/drinks: Kombucha beverages/drinks...
- Mushroom processed milk: Kefir Yogurt
- High-end new exclusive king lobster mushroom....

Figure 5: Emmay's line-up of mushroom products.

Smiley Mushroom.[2] The brand has been operating since 2010, carrying various green products, including processed foods and beverages. In 2019, Emmay expanded its offerings, producing alternative protein products for pork, and it continues to extend to beef, chicken, and seafood (see Figure 5).

Insights and Challenges

Running a family business and a start-up is very different, as Van has discovered. She grappled with taxes, certification fees, and other monthly fixed costs. Once again, she educated herself on business taxes and laws to meet these challenges head-on. She believes it is crucial to familiarize oneself with the business before starting one. Therefore, she took many classes to learn as she believes they are essential to running a business, though her greatest learning took place on the job.

---

[2] https://www.technavio.com/report/global-canned-mushroom-market-industry-analysis?tnplus.

Building a team was crucial to Van's success. She recommends having at least one other team member, perhaps a co-founder. Going solo has been extremely difficult for her as she lacked support. In the future, Emmay plans to recruit more talent and raise more funds through VCs as it aspires to become the dominant player in the alternative protein industry in Vietnam within the next five years.

Emmay's in-house team comprises 39 employees, up from just eight in 2021. To help its expansion in Vietnam, these managers and C-level hires are deployed across the sales and marketing, finance, production, R&D, and logistics departments.

Overcoming Obstacles

While the idea behind fungi technology has proven to be a practical solution, Emmay's goal could only be fulfilled with proper funding. With a growing market for alternative meats, it was clear to investors that the company was riding the crest of a strong wave.

Just as importantly, Emmay had a winning product, an excellent solution to the problem, and a strategy backed by research. However, the road to securing funding was still an arduous one. Ms. Pham had to prove her business was worth taking a chance on, and she had to learn how to run a business while developing the product concurrently.

When the global COVID-19 pandemic reached Vietnam in 2020, everyday business operations became challenging due to strict health protocols and supply chain delays. Unfortunately, these issues also affected many businesses across the globe.

Having a lack of resources might be a blessing in disguise as you never know where the process might take you. Fewer resources spell a greater need for more creativity and resourcefulness.
— **Ms. Pham Hong Van**, Founder and CEO of Emmay

Ms. Pham sourced for investors in many ways — one of which was to pitch her case for women's empowerment. She decided to look for specific grants that supported female-run businesses.

Looking Ahead

The company is looking to increase the number of retail points and distributors in the Vietnamese market by 2025 (see Figure 6). It aims to secure at least USD7-10 million worth of investment funds before expanding to more international markets.

In the next five years, I want Emmay to be the key player in the alternative protein market in Vietnam and other regions.
— Ms. **Pham Hong Van**, Founder and CEO of Emmay

From 2022 to 2025, Emmay plans to concentrate on key markets like Singapore, China, Taiwan, and Hong Kong, establishing 100–2,000 retail

- 2024 – 2025: Expand to UAE, India
- 100 retail points - 1000 retail points
- Only expand continuously after raising funds next round successfully
- Fundraising: $20M USD - $40M USD

- 2023 – 2025: Expand to Japan, South Korea
- 100 retail points - 1000 retail points

- 2022 – 2025: Expand to Singapore, China, Taiwan, Hong Kong
- 100 retail points - 2000 retail points

- +500 retail points in Vietnam in 2021
- 2022 - 2025: +3000 retail points in MT channel and +200 distributors in GT channels
- Fundrasing: $7M USD - $10M USD

Figure 6: Emmay's growth projections.

points in each country. After that, it intends to tap into the Japanese and South Korean markets, where it plans to set up at least 100–1,000 retail points. Next will be an expansion into the United Arab Emirates (UAE) and EU from 2023 to 2025.

Within the next five years, Emmy hopes to get between USD20–30 million in investments to support any future expansion.

CHAPTER 10

Maptionnaire: Building Cities Together Through Collaboration and Engagement

I n 2005, Dr. Maarit Kahila realized that many urban planners were open to collaborating with citizens and in using soft data obtained from residents in their planning and development work. This realization has largely informed her doctoral research on participatory planning at Aalto University in Finland and later served as a guide in her entrepreneurial journey.

In 2011, Dr. Kahila and four other researchers came together to set up Maptionnaire, a company that is on a mission to create more "livable and lovable" urban environments. Dr. Kahila and her fellow founders devised a piece of software to solve the communication problem between residents and planners. Today, the Maptionnaire Community Engagement Platform enables citizens and urban planners to work together more efficiently.

Maptionnaire supports urban planners in realizing participation and engagement projects by providing them with geolocated data collection and communication tools. The platform streamlines the community engagement process, facilitating collaboration between urban planners and citizens, allowing for a more accessible gathering of insights to change cities.

Maptionnaire has come a long way since its beginning. Three of its initial co-founders have left the company, and Dr. Kahila and Dr. Anna Broberg solely run the operations. They alternate the CEO role between them to distribute the responsibilities evenly and have a board of advisors that provide invaluable business insights to them. They have also recruited 11 indispensable employees to boost the efficacy of its business operations.

Problem and Opportunity: The Problem with City Planning

During her time in academia, Dr. Kahila received requests from planners to utilize the software she had co-developed for public participation in other projects. This was the defining moment when she realized that she might have stumbled upon an idea that would solve a major problem among urban planners — involving residents in the planning process.

We were not keen to become entrepreneurs.
— **Dr. Maarit Kahila and Dr. Anna Broberg**, Co-founders
of Maptionnaire

Dr. Kahila and Dr. Broberg were keen on pursuing a business venture because they wanted to create more impact by taking the technology further. However, to do so, they had to juggle between completing their Ph.D. work and running the company.

During their time in academia, they found that changing the way cities were developed required more than what academia provided. It needed a commercial approach as well. Just like that, Maptionnaire was born.

Impact and change cannot happen through just research projects. We had to give them a tool.

Need for Public Engagement and Inputs

The rapid growth in city areas has created a gap between the local communities and decision-makers. To build better functioning cities, various stakeholders should be involved in decision-making or consulted for their opinions. After all, cities are built by people, for people.

Community engagement workshops are popular avenues for urban planners to involve citizens and uncover opportunities for collaboration. While in-person community workshops nurture a dialog between residents and planners through a creative problem-solving process, it is often a tedious and a non-inclusive process.

These in-person workshops required organizers to sort through multiple post-it notes and filter out some of the potential ideas brought in by the community. But, with post-it notes often covering the walls, how does one ensure they do not miss out on the best game-changers?

What's more, such workshops are often attended by the same few citizens. This is because it is difficult to reach out to all stakeholders, let alone involve them in decision-making by attending in-person meetings. Workshops require stakeholders to commit time and effort to participate. As such, ideas contributed by the same few people tend only to fulfill a smaller community's needs instead of the community at large.

We keep arranging these face-to-face workshops (that are a traditional way of collaboration and community engagement), although today's world is very digital. It's very instant; everyone has their mobile phones in their hands... and during this pandemic, we have been forced to turn our eyes on how to do this type of work more digitally in the future.
— **Dr. Maarit Kahila**, Co-founder of Maptionnaire

The world today is digital, instant, and collaborative. Therefore, traditional face-to-face collaboration and community engagement methods need to be digitized to reach out to more stakeholders.

Solution
Getting People Digitally Engaged

To digitally transform how public opinions are collected, Maptionnaire introduced an online community engagement platform. With this platform, planners get all the tools they need for arranging community engagement processes online — for everyone, anywhere.

Community Engagement Platform

Maptionnaire was designed to be a one-stop community engagement platform for receiving valuable insights and managing public participation and engagement processes (see Figure 1). It engages the community by gathering insights, interpreting, analyzing, collaborating, and sharing the results with decision-makers and urban planners.

This helps to not only build trust but also make better decisions that benefit the community. More importantly, it enables extensive public opinions to be accounted for in a large-scale and actionable manner.

Figure 1: Maptionnaire's community engagement platform.

The platform works in four spheres:

(1) **Questionnaire Design and Data Collection**: Maptionnaire enables urban planners to create map-based questionnaires, polls, and surveys to gather geographic information system (GIS) data provided by citizens. A participatory budgeting process can give stakeholders some control over how public funds should be spent.

(2) **Results Measurement and Information Analysis**: Maptionnaire allows urban planners to analyze and visualize GIS data, define engagement key performance indicators (KPIs), report the outcomes, and even transfer data for further analysis.

(3) **Project Communication and Planning**: Maptionnaire facilitates communication and discussions between stakeholders on dedicated webpages. Urban planners can create their project pages and engagement portfolio, deliver statutory feedback, and archive information for future use.

(4) **Collaboration**: Maptionnaire helps urban planners share information across departments, manage users and projects, compile an organization's engagement activities, and foster discussion with citizens.

To help urban planners achieve tangible results in these four spheres of activities, Maptionnaire offers seven modules on its platform:

(1) **Design, Collect and Analyze**: Design, Collect, and Analyze constitutes Maptionnaire's core module. It allows urban planners to reach out to an extensive network of stakeholders and collect good-quality data based on map-based and picture-based questionnaires. Maptionnaire has a built-in translation tool — planners can translate every questionnaire into the languages used by target audiences and view

the original and translated text side-by-side to minimize translation errors. With analytical tools, urban planners can get visual analysis to better interpret the questionnaire results.

(2) **Gamified Decision–Making**: Gamified Decision-Making allows urban planners to build budgeting questionnaires using a map. This empowers citizens by giving them the flexibility to decide on resource allocation in a fun and engaging way. Such voting tools improve interactions and allow citizens to better indicate their preferences. Notably, it is about co-creating and having citizens weigh the possible options and trade-offs in planning decisions.

(3) **Webpage Builder**: Webpage Builder allows urban planners to create a webpage to communicate with various stakeholders. Urban planners could leverage this tool to provide up-to-date project plans that serve as a social sharing platform for discussion and feedback gathering.

(4) **3D Collaboration**: 3D Collaboration allows urban planners to integrate 3D models for buildings or living environments with their questionnaires. Making buildings or living environments come to life improves project clarity and helps citizens better visualize complex development projects.

(5) **Automated Public Hearing Process**: An Automated Public Hearing Process allows urban planners to automate the documentation process with standardized or customized formats based on an organization's needs. Besides making documentation easier, it makes the process more transparent for citizens who can easily request a copy of the document.

(6) **Real-Time Feedback Map**: A Real-Time Feedback Map allows urban planners to instantaneously gather feedback from citizens. As a result, citizens' feedback is immediately delivered to urban planners and integrated into their maintenance system. This helps urban planners to wisely allocate more time for important tasks.

(7) **Participatory Budgeting Process**: Planners can run the whole Participatory Budgeting Process with Maptionnaire — from idea collection to presenting the winning proposals. Participatory budgeting turns citizens into decision-makers, giving them the power to influence resource allocation in their city or area.

Urban planners can develop surveys and project pages to gather information from key stakeholders and design better city-living solutions for their citizens. This includes how citizens perceive their living environment, what they value most in their living environment, and even their movements within or across cities. Ultimately, Maptionnaire wants to support public participation efforts for urban planners to build better, functional cities for their citizens.

The Business Model
Target Market
Urban planning organizations, design consultancies, cities and local governments, communication agencies, universities and research institutions, and energy companies working on city development projects are important stakeholders and partners for Maptionnaire. The project areas include urban planning and design, transportation and mobility, infrastructure, buildings, parks and recreation, energy, public health, sustainability, and nature.

Affirmation
Since its incorporation in 2011, Maptionnaire has been utilized in almost 10,000 projects globally for community engagement. As a result, Maptionnaire has garnered over 300 active customers from over 40 countries. In addition, the company has established solid geographical

footprints in the Nordics, Benelux, Germany, the United Kingdom, the United States, and Canada.

Some of the notable projects concluded with the help of the Maptionnaire community engagement platform include "Gathering Traffic Safety Experiences at the World's Largest Amateur Bike Race" in Sweden, "Digitalizing Community Engagement in Vantaa" and "Walkability Survey in Helsinki" in Finland, and "Denver Investing in Inclusive Digital Participation" in the USA.

Here's what several organizations have to say about working with Maptionnaire:

An online platform like Maptionnaire can be incredibly helpful in reaching a broader, more diverse group of residents that better reflects the community in your city.
— **Lizzie Friend**, Data Analytics & Informatics Manager for Denver

Whoever is looking for a map-based online participation tool will end up choosing Maptionnaire in the end. We don't know of any solution that even comes close to what Maptionnaire has to offer.
— Urbanista, Germany

Revenue Model

The Maptionnaire Community Engagement Platform adopts a usage-based subscription model. Users can purchase a fixed-term subscription of 12 months or less or a continuous subscription that includes technical support and training. Prices range from €500 to €4,000 per month, depending on the selected subscription level. Maptionnaire is a browser-based software, so its users do not need to install any additional software or apps to access the service.

There are three different subscription plans for users to pick from:

(1) **Collect:** *Collect* is an essential toolkit for urban planners who require map-based community engagement. It comes with Maptionnaire's core module features of the Design, Collect, and Analyze module.

(2) **Communicate:** *Communicate* is targeted at urban planners requiring effective communication. The standard toolkit for building map-based surveys is enriched with a Webpage Builder for running all community engagement activities in one place.

(3) **Innovate:** *Innovate* is targeted at urban planners looking for the full community engagement experience, including participatory budgeting.

Furthermore, there is flexibility to purchase add-on modules with any chosen subscription plan. These include *Teams* for easy information sharing within organizations, *Reporting Dashboard* for viewing visual reports, *Real-Time Feedback Map, 3D Collaboration,* and *Automized Public Hearing Process.*

Insights

Despite creating a well-sought-after product, the university was not keen to work on the continual development of the service. According to Dr. Kahila, universities may be eager to innovate, but they are not enthusiastic about developing, updating, and maintaining software. This meant that taking Maptionnaire to the next level would require conviction and a lot of grit.

While Dr. Kahila was running a project in a Finnish city in her capacity as a university researcher, she unexpectedly received an irritated phone call from a union leader in that city. With a raised voice, the union leader was questioning everything that Dr. Kahila was doing in community engagement and her motives for conducting surveys in the city. The leader claimed to know everything about the city and that there was no need for whatever Dr. Kahila did.

This episode revitalized Dr. Kahila's purpose and strengthened her resolve. She aimed to change and improve how things were done in urban planning and citizen engagement.

She also realized that the impact she wanted to achieve required her to start a company because researchers often lacked the power to enact change around how the industry operated. She came to the conclusion that she had to create a universal tool to allow planners to independently initiate their projects without the company's guidance. More than an impact, Maptionnaire strove for universal change.

Notably, the founders of Maptionnaire are geographers and academics. They had no business skills and had lots to learn at the start. "I'm a geographer. No business skills whatsoever," said Dr. Kahila. "We're still learning. By doing, listening, reading."

In the early stages, the team operated with the presumption that they, as researchers, knew the best practice for gathering data. Unfortunately, this turned out to be a big problem. "We weren't listening carefully," admitted Dr. Kahila.

They initially designed a set of ready templates into their software to gather people's opinions and ideas only to realize that the business world was very different. Planners told them that the questions were too academic and impractical. With that feedback, the team changed the way they made decisions.

As a female entrepreneur in an IT world led by men, Dr. Kahila faced many hardships in her long and arduous journey to success. She attributed her success to her self-belief and her trust that she would be able to overcome any difficulty, no matter how impossible it might seem. She also firmly believed in learning to tune out the white noise when receiving advice from others.

"If you do not know what you are doing and are not confident, self-doubt will quickly start creeping inside of you, and you start to get the feeling that you might not be able to do this at all," she said. Instead of listening to every bit of advice, she believes that nothing beats executing a plan and letting it do the talking.

Looking Ahead

In 2017, the urban planning software industry was valued at around €2 billion, and cloud geographic information system (GIS) is projected to be a $5.2 billion market by 2026.[1] With Maptionnaire being broadly recognized as a community engagement platform for urban planning, it is well positioned to capitalize on its success and become a major player in its industry. It aims to grow the business by focusing more closely on the existing target markets, exploring new markets, and keeping current customers happy and engaged with the service.

Over the past decade, Maptionnaire has helped urban planners build smart cities with smart communities. Primarily focused on government technology, civil solutions, and cybersecurity sectors, Maptionnaire continues to transform how public opinions are solicited for urban planning with its map-based community engagement platform.

---

[1] Technavio, GeoBuiz 2017, Frost & Sullivan, Grand View Research.

CHAPTER 11
Summary and Conclusion

E ntrepreneurs are not born, they are made, so goes the saying. Either way, some entrepreneurs seem to possess the right combination of traits that, combined with their life experience and personal circumstances, shape them into what they are today. In writing this book, we wanted to tell the personal stories of the founders of nine start-ups from around the world — on how, through their resilience and tenacity, they brought their companies through countless challenges and problems, trials, and tribulations. They emerged much stronger than when they first started.

The common threads among several of the start-ups featured in this book are an experience of prior hardship, a sense of social justice, being at the right place at the right time, daring to try, visionary leadership, and having a sheer sense of conviction and grit. Several founders have highly technical backgrounds — they are on a constant lookout for new market opportunities that can capitalize on and harness their technical capabilities to churn out products that are not only useful but can also better serve customers and meet specific needs.

The founders in this book share a common vision of bringing about change in their industries to achieve better outcomes for their customers and stakeholders. They also managed to find financial and technical resources to back up their ambition. Many of them have relied heavily on their networks and the support of like-minded people to get their businesses off the ground.

In each case, the start-ups in this book were able to overcome obstacles and build dynamically growing companies. They know that success is not a given and that hard work and dedication are required. They each discovered that there are no shortcuts — you need to put in the work and continuously improve your product or service to get a chance to be successful.

Finally, the entrepreneurs featured in this book know the importance of "thinking outside the box" — they have all taken different paths to success and have made a name for their businesses by tapping into undiscovered or neglected market opportunities or adopting innovative business models.

Here are some of the specific themes we encountered:

Prior Hardship

Ms. Or Litman founded Eyelight because of what she went through as a child. She experienced emotional pain when she witnessed her diabetic grandfather losing his eyesight. Her love for her grandfather spurred her to find a solution to help blind or near-blind people "see" by substituting the sense of sight with touch and hearing. This allows such individuals to better navigate their surroundings, participate in e-commerce, and enjoy entertainment. In short, they can achieve a level of independence that they previously were not able to attain.

Litman and her co-founder, Omer Gohary, managed to secure funding to successfully launch their pilot product. Being a first mover has its advantages — Eyelight, headquartered in Israel, is poised to capture a significant slice of a market worth USD7.4 billion by 2026 that is growing at an annual compounded rate of 8.5% over the next several years. Its product not only allows blind and partially sighted people to build their confidence but it also helps them achieve personal independence and be socially included.

Another company, Emmay, was founded as a result of hardship and bankruptcy. In her earlier years, Ms. Pham Hong Van's family suffered bankruptcy — it was a tough time but through sheer grit and perseverance, they turned the humble shiitake mushroom from their family kitchen into mushroom floss that lifted the family out of financial ruin into a global sustainable business. The company, which Van founded in 2017 in Vietnam, expanded quickly from only mushroom-based products to a broad product line of plant-based instant foods and alternative sustainable proteins by harnessing green technologies.

Today, the company has hundreds of retail shops and thousands of other retail outlets in Vietnam. It has also established itself in the EU and Asia, particularly in the major regions of China, Hong Kong, Japan, Korea, Singapore, and Taiwan. In addition, its products are available through online platforms. To get a sense of the sheer size of the burgeoning market, it is noted that the alternative meat industry was slated to grow at an annual compounded rate of 10% from 2019 through 2029 to USD140 billion. Today, Emmay offers alternative meat products for pork, beef, chicken, and seafood. It plans to continue expanding its product offerings and retail points across existing and new markets.

Sense of Social Justice

During his youth, Dr. Jonathan Ng, the founder of Iterative Scopes, originally from Singapore, now living in the USA, had the opportunity to visit war-torn Cambodia in the aftermath of the Khmer Rouge regime. What struck him most was the dismal state of the country's hospitals, particularly those in rural areas. He was deeply moved by the inequality in healthcare access between the rich and the poor. Dedicated to improving healthcare for the underprivileged, particularly children in Cambodia, he set out to fulfill a lifelong mission of creating healthcare innovations for the disadvantaged.

Jon, as he is known to his friends, went to medical school in Singapore and then pursued an MBA from MIT and MPA in healthcare policy from Harvard University to further train for his life's calling. Alongside his philanthropic work among the children in Cambodia, the healthcare entrepreneur started Iterative Scopes — a company specializing in computational gastroenterology, which utilizes AI technology to provide doctors with quicker detection and diagnosis for their patients. The company serves the gastrointestinal market, worth more than USD7 billion and growing annually at a compounded rate of 8.5%. The software developed by Iterative Scopes is currently used in around 300 centers across the USA. The company has since raised around USD200 million in funding and employs more than 170 employees. With annual revenue in excess of USD5 million, the company is primed for further growth as Jon aims to improve global access to high-quality medical care and eliminate disparities in healthcare outcomes.

Right Place at the Right Time

Being at the right place at the right time is especially important, particularly for start-ups with ideas that have medical/healthcare applications. Dr. Hongjie Liu met her co-founder of Reexen, Dr. Xiaofeng Yang, when they were both pursuing their master's degrees in integrated circuit design in Singapore. Subsequently, both went on to conduct research for their doctoral studies — Hongjie focused on neuroinformatics in Zurich, Switzerland, and Xiaofeng on analog circuit design in Macau, China.

Amid her research, Dr. Liu saw a budding need for low-power energy-efficient integrated chips that utilize mixed signal computing in their chip design.

Reexen was founded in 2018 in China to develop revolutionary chip architecture that integrates analog sensing with digital computing. This technology is high on energy but low on power consumption; its design allows for the flexible distribution of computing power, thereby speeding up computing time and lengthening battery life. Its chips are reshaping AI-based hardware and can be used in robots, biomedical sensors, earphones, smart wearable devices, IP cameras, and autonomous vehicles. To date, Reexen has raised about USD20 million in funding and generated revenues of USD7 million in 2022. The company, which also has an office in Switzerland, expects to receive orders worth more than USD40 million by 2024 and expand its offerings in Europe, China, and the USA. To support this impending growth, the founders plan to increase the number of employees from 70 to 300 in the near future.

Another team of Ph.D. holders chanced upon an exciting market opportunity to supply stem cells in sufficient numbers consistently while pursuing their doctoral research on 3D microtissue engineering. CytoNiche co-founders Dr. Xiaojun Yan and Dr. Wei Liu worked with their adviser at Tsinghua University, Professor Yanan Du, to bring their idea to fruition. From undergraduate studies in chemical and biomolecular engineering from Singapore to a Ph.D. from a top school in China, these two co-founders are ready to fill a pressing need from biotechnology and pharmaceutical companies to supply high-quality cells for use in cell and gene therapy. They quickly realized the real need was in the production process, i.e., how the stem cell drugs were made using live cell cultures.

Today, CytoNiche, which is headquartered in Beijing, China, focuses on regenerative medicine that utilizes cell and genetic therapies in the treatment of patients. Since 2018, the company raised more than

USD60 million in funding and invested in sizeable R&D and production facilities in Beijing and Tianjin in China. It has secured more than 60 patents and is considered the first to launch pharmaceutical-grade products, giving it a distinct advantage over its competitors. The company currently supplies over 50% of China's stem cell therapy companies. It is targeting the global regenerative medicine market, which is forecasted to be worth USD40 billion by 2027 and is growing at a compounded annual rate of 11–15%.

Dare to Try

Some entrepreneurs have found it worth their while to abandon their dream of an advanced academic degree in exchange for something, in their mind, infinitely more valuable — the creation of an exciting new start-up. It's now or never! Siddharth Jadhav, the founder of Polybee, gave up on his ambition of pursuing a Ph.D. in aerodynamics when he chanced, by accident, upon the idea of agricultural innovation by developing "smart" mechanical bees to pollinate crops that can improve food security for the vulnerable. A book on the evolutionary history of human beings, which he picked up during his downtime, contained a message that sparked in him the zeal to want to do something for the world's most vulnerable people by enhancing their food security. That was good, but as an aerodynamics engineer, Siddharth knew next to nothing about agriculture. How then could he realize his goal?

Siddharth received financial support from the National University of Singapore, where he worked as a research engineer, to explore his initial ideas. Subsequently, the Temasek Foundation, a Singapore-based non-profit organization, provided him with a small plot of land to test out his prototypes. The world was facing a production deficit due to a dire lack of natural pollinators due to factors such as climate change and the urbanization of cities. Siddharth drew on his background in aerodynamics to develop micro-drones for the autonomous pollination of crops rather than depending on bees. For context, the United Nations had estimated that the market for fresh produce was worth around USD850 billion in 2022. Efficient pollination has the potential to stimulate the fresh produce market to reach its full capacity of USD2.5 trillion.

Headquartered in Singapore, Polybee has built autonomous micro-drones that can cover a large area in a timely and consistent manner with a margin of error of 1 cm. These drones have computer vision to navigate autonomously and have a 90% success rate in turning flowers into fruits. In 2022, the technology was shown to increase crop yield by 50% compared to traditional bumblebee pollination. The company generates revenues through a usage-based subscription model, which allows its customers to have better control over their costs and provides them with more flexibility to align their costs with consumption.

Another promising entrepreneur, Justin Liu of ZhenRobotics, was deep into his Ph.D. studies in Computer Science in Switzerland when he decided to withdraw from it to pursue his interest in robotics and artificial intelligence. The company was established in 2016 to develop service robots that revolutionize last-mile delivery, mobile security patrol, and unmanned robotic cleaning. The solutions that the company provides are aimed at enabling cities to become smarter, sustainable, and resilient. The COVID-19 pandemic accelerated ZhenRobotics' business from one highly reliant on humans — such as those in the service industry like food and logistics deliveries, housekeeping and cleaning, security and surveillance, and common retail — to one that minimizes human contact.

ZhenRobotics uses robots to address China's two-pronged problem of rising labor costs and a shrinking labor force. Each of its robots is embedded with its five core technologies: machine learning, computer vision, electronic systems, autonomous localization, and navigation. Its delivery robot can even use ultraviolet light to disinfect its delivery parcels. The company's patrol robot can secure premises through real-time visual inspection of public spaces with 5G and AI traceability. The robots not only clean but also purify the air. ZhenRobotics is developing more service applications and inventions, all of which provide for a smarter and cleaner unmanned service environment at a reduced cost. Thus far, its robot sales have earned the company margins over 50–70% and increased its client companies' profits by more than USD20,000 a year per robot, on average. With the service robot market projected to be worth USD5 billion in China and USD14.5 billion globally, the sky is the limit for ZhenRobotics.

Visionary Leadership

After realizing how saturated the market for medical robotics was, Dr. Atif Syed, founder of England-based Wootzano, capitalized on the robotics technology that he had developed to apply to the agricultural industry to reduce the heavy manpower requirements in the industry. In 2016, armed with a freshly minted Ph.D., Dr. Syed, who holds a doctorate in engineering and bionanotechnology, started Wootzano to use robots for fruit and vegetable sorting, picking, and labeling. Atif's robots are unique — they have hands covered with electronic skin to do the work of three human beings in a day. The robots have hands with the necessary dexterity and computer vision to pick the right fruits at the correct degree of ripeness and ensure that the soft and delicate produce is not damaged or bruised. This is especially important for produce such as grapes and tomatoes. Wootzano's technology increases productivity and sustainability in the supply chain by reducing food wastage and improving food security.

The company's sophisticated AI technology provided a ready solution to fruit-picking and packing companies, particularly during the

COVID-19 pandemic when margins went up by more than 4%. The dexterity of the robots is particularly attractive to industry players for revolutionizing the market. The icing on the cake is that Wootzano priced its robots so that customers get their money back within 12 months or earlier. It is working on orders worth more than £100 million and has already signed a contract worth over £300 million to cover the UK and European markets. It will next target more markets in Europe, Australia, North America, and South Africa.

Conviction and Grit

In the midst of completing their Ph.D. degrees, Dr. Maarit Kahila and Dr. Anna Broberg, co-founders of Maptionnaire, ran an urban planning platform that streamlines the community engagement process to facilitate collaboration between a city's urban planners and their citizens. The Finland-based company's mission is to create more livable and lovable urban environments through its software, designed to facilitate better communication between a city's residents and its planners. Its stakeholders include urban planning organizations, design consultancies, cities and local governments, communication agencies, universities and research institutions, and energy companies working on city development projects.

Maptionnaire's software has been used in around 10,000 global projects and has customers from more than 40 countries. The company has a particularly strong presence in the Nordics and has established a footprint elsewhere in Europe and North America. The company generates revenues through a usage-based subscription model where access to its services is through browser-based software. Depending on the type of services required, prices can range from EUR500 to EUR4,000 a month. The urban planning software industry is valued at over EUR2 billion. With its growing cloud geographic information system (GIS) market,

Maptionnaire continues its quest to help urban planners build smart cities with smart communities.

Concluding Remarks

The stories depicted in the preceding chapters offer exciting prospects for a smart, sustainable, and resilient future. These founders' determination and hard work demonstrate that, with passion, commitment, and resilience, even the most daring ideas can be achieved. The entrepreneurial human spirit enables novel technologies to flourish in a viable and successful business for those willing to take risks and work hard to build their unique dreams.

All nine start-ups featured in this book made it to the finals of the 10th Lee Kuan Yew Global Business Plan Competition (LKYGBPC) as recognition of their promising business prospects. Several of them won special prizes:

- Iterative Scopes won the Lee Kuan Yew BETA Grand Prize and the Best Presentation Prize.
- CytoNiche won the Best Professor–Student Team Prize and the Sino-Singapore Nanjing Eco Hi-Tech Island Investment Prize.
- Polybee won the DBS Tech for Impact Prize and the Wavemaker Partners Enterprise Start-up Award.

Iterative Scopes, Polybee, Wootzano, and ZhenRobotics were among the select few awarded the NSCC Supercomputing Resource Prize.

We hope that the stories of these successful entrepreneurs encourage readers to follow in their footsteps and perhaps even enter future LKYGBPC competitions. We wish the aspiring entrepreneurs and business students all the best and trust that they will dare to take the first step in realizing their dreams through commitment and dedication.

References

Cooper, A., Gimeno-Gascon, J., & Woo, C. (1994). Initial human and financial capital as predictors of new venture performance. *Journal of Business Venturing*, 9(5), 371–395.

Djankov, S., Qian, Y., Roland, G., & Zhuravskaya, E. (2006). Who are China's entrepreneurs? *American Economic Review*, 96(2), 348–352.

Gans, J. S. & Stern, S. (2003). The product market and the market for "ideas": Commercialization strategies for technology entrepreneurs. *Research Policy*, 32(2), 333–350.

Harari, Y. N. (2014). *Sapiens: A Brief History of Humankind*, New York: Random House.

Haynie, J. M., Shepherd, D. A., & Patzelt, H. (2012). Cognitive adaptability and an entrepreneurial task: The role of metacognitive ability and feedback. *Entrepreneurship Theory and Practice*, 36(2), 237–265.

Howell, S. T. (2021). Learning from feedback: Evidence from new ventures. *Review of Finance*, 25(3), 595–627.

Mooradian, T., Matzler, K., Uzelac, B., & Bauer, F. (2016). Perspiration and inspiration: Grit and innovativeness as antecedents of entrepreneurial success. *Journal of Economic Psychology*, 56, 232–243.

Politis, D. (2005). The process of entrepreneurial learning: A conceptual framework. *Entrepreneurship Theory and Practice*, 29(4), 399–424.

Romanelli, E. (1989). Environments and strategies of organizational start up: Effects on early survival. *Administrative Science Quarterly*, 34, 369–387.

Schumpeter, J. A. (1934). *The Theory of Economic Development*. Cambridge, MA: Harvard University Press.

Shane, S. (2000). Prior knowledge and the discovery of entrepreneurial opportunities. *Organization Science*, 11(4), 448–469.

Shepherd, D. A. (2003). Learning from business failure: Propositions of grief recovery for the self-employed. *Academy of Management Review*, 28(2), 318–328.

Shepherd, D. A. & DeTienne, D. R. (2005). Prior knowledge, potential financial reward, and opportunity identification. *Entrepreneurship Theory and Practice*, 29(1), 91–112.

Song, M., Podoynitsyna, K., van der Bij, H., & Halman, J. (2008). Success factors in new ventures: A meta-analysis. *Journal of Product Innovation Management*, 25(1), 7–27.

Ucbasaran, D., Wright, M., & Westhead, P. (2008). Opportunity identification and pursuit: Does an entrepreneur's human capital matter? *Small Business Economics*, 30, 153–173.

Wright, R. W. & Dana, L. P. (2003). Changing paradigms of international entrepreneurship strategy. *Journal of International Entrepreneurship*, 1(1), 135–152.

Index